The
Dilemmas
Of
Journalism

Speaking for Myself

The
Dilemmas
Of
Journalism

GERALD PRIESTLAND

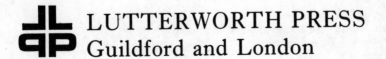 LUTTERWORTH PRESS
Guildford and London

First published in 1979

By the same author:
America – The Changing Nation (Eyre & Spottiswoode, 1968)
Frying Tonight (Gentry Books Ltd, 1971)
The Future of Violence (Hamish Hamilton Ltd, 1976)
Yours Faithfully (Collins Fount, 1979)

ISBN 0 7188 2394 X

Set in 11/13 pt Imprint
Set, printed and bound in Great Britain by
Fakenham Press Limited,
Fakenham, Norfolk.

Contents

Introduction

The book that follows is based on a pair of lectures – 'Journalism and Terrorism' and 'The Moral Dilemmas of Journalism' – developed over the past few years and delivered at various church and academic occasions in the United States and Britain. I am grateful to all those who have sat through them and contributed to the discussion of them.

I am grateful, as ever, to the BBC which has provided me with the employment and experience upon which my conclusions are based. Where I may appear to be critical of broadcasting in Britain, there is nothing I have not been permitted to say publicly before. There is no question of this being either an authorised version or a piece of protest literature. Nor is it intended to be a blast at my many hard-working and able colleagues in the media. They have quite enough to put up with, without having to feel they should worry about sniping from me. One or two have already commented that I am presenting a theology of journalism rather than a practical handbook, a statement of how things ought to be rather than a realistic appraisal of what can actually be done. They may have a point here. But for me there would be no moral dilemmas in journalism if this tension did not exist.

For this is an avowedly religious book. I have tried to make it clear that there is no reason why a Christian's journalism should be better than anybody else's – though in some ways it may be different. Perhaps it is more surprising that a Christian should be a journalist at all. For if the mass media are really as sensational, trivial, irresponsible, unprincipled, distorting and corrupting as many prominent churchpeople consider them to be, then a Christian should no more be a journalist than a drug dealer or pornographer.

1

In his 1976 lectures on *Christ and the Media*, Malcolm Muggeridge put the case against my profession most eloquently.

> Future historians will surely see us as having created in the media a Frankenstein monster who no one knows how to control or direct, and marvel that we should have so meekly subjected ourselves to its destructive and often malign influence . . . Supposing there had been a fourth temptation when our Lord encountered the devil in the wilderness – this time an offer of networked TV appearances, in prime time, to proclaim and expound his Gospel?

Malcolm has no doubt whatever that our Lord would have turned down flat the world of fantasy that broadcasting projects.

Myself, I am not so sure. It seems to me that with the Sermon on the Mount, preaching from a boat, his entry into Jerusalem spectacular plus the purging of the temple, Jesus showed himself a master of mass communication (as indeed has Malcolm Muggeridge). But to balance the argument – and broadcasters are only held to be objective when their statements cancel themselves out like this – let me quote from the final statement of the 1977 National Evangelical Anglican Congress at Nottingham, 'The nation', it says in part, 'is well served by all branches of the media, which offer many instances of profoundly positive, life-enriching and entertaining productions. Many people would agree that the good far outweighs the bad in terms of quantity . . .'

And again the statement, which was drafted under the leadership of the Director of the Festival of Light, confesses, 'For far too long we have failed to exercise a sympathetic appreciation of the pressures under which many individuals in the media are operating. We have been too quick to criticise harshly out of ignorance, and we acknowledge it to our shame . . . We are gladdened to see many Christian men and women heeding the challenge to enter a career of whole-hearted professionalism in the world of the mass media.' Amen to that, and it was a pity Malcolm Muggeridge was not there to join in.

2

Which is not to say that I myself have been swept away on a wave of evangelical optimism. I have had to face profound and continuous doubts about my occupation as a newsman – for that is what I am, first and foremost. Although at present I work within the religious broadcasting department of the BBC I am not an ordained minister or a lay preacher; I have not even studied theology, let alone been trained in pastoral care. I am a journalist.

But I also happen to be a Quaker, a member of the Religious Society of Friends, and I find this central to what I do and why I am doing it. Quakers are, of course, pacifists; and that means not merely non-fighters but peace*makers*. It seems to me that Jesus was also, and it is gratifying to Quakers today to find that the other churches are scrapping more and more of the doctrine of the just war and turning to Christian pacificsm. It also seems to me that the only substitute for war, perhaps the only defence against it, is communication; and that a journalist can do real service to the cause of peace by hurrying to and fro between the various groups into which men divide themselves, carrying their messages, finding out what they really mean and want and explaining one group to another.

Quakers are bidden to 'walk cheerfully over the world, answering that of God in every man'. And since they believe that there *is* something of God in every man they should, as journalists, be very slow to dismiss anyone as not worth listening to. They should be slow to condemn, optimistic about the chances of understanding. But, working as they have often done amidst the wreckage of war and disaster, they should not underestimate the number of times it may be necessary to pick oneself up and start all over again.

For it seems to me that with all their faults and dangers, the liberal values of a free press as we know it today are still worth defending. That press, and broadcasting, are not immutable in shape – nothing is. But it also seems to me that the free media of today are being threatened with destruction rather than change. They are being forced backwards over a cliff with a blindfold over their eyes, and far too many responsible people – especially church people – are indifferent or even cheerful at the prospect.

3

The mass media are as sinful as any other human institution; though I believe that their principal errors – over-simplification, incestuousness, technical over-smartness and a lack of contact with their public – are not those commonly emphasised. Those who criticise the media and call for 'something to be done about them' have far too little understanding of how they really work. They don't understand how much the media are at the mercy of rising costs, of sources who will not tell the truth, and of a society whose homes and schools are no longer Christian. I would urge, not that Christians should redouble their reproaches from the sidelines, but that they should roll up their sleeves and come to grips with mass communication themselves.

1. Catalogue of Woe

The Bishop of Southwark no longer turns on the early morning radio news in bed. 'Life', he told his people, 'is difficult enough without having to listen to a catalogue of disasters and crimes as soon as I open my eyes.'

The bishop went on to complain that although his diocese was full of dedicated and law-abiding citizens, rarely a word was said about them in the media until one of them blotted his copybook and hit the headlines. Worse still was the emphasis on crime and violence on the television. Instead of being purveyors of gloom, despondency and evil, it was up to the mass media to assist the nation's spiritual renewal by purveying 'true patriotism and great achievement'.

Now there is not an editor in the land who would not be delighted to blanket his front page with patriotic achievements, if only he could learn of them. The short answer to the bishop is that we may all assume that people are doing what they are *meant* to be doing without it appearing in the media. But news is what is exceptional; and if the nation or the church want exceptionally good news, then they must go out and make it.

Yet there is no denying that many hundreds of thousands of people will agree with the bishop. They are increasingly tempted to get something done about the media by legislation. They are not quite sure *what* should be done, or how, but they are convinced that the media could be better than they are. So they could. But they could also be much worse, in subtler, more dangerous ways, and that is the biggest argument for leaving what we may still call our 'free' press alone to take care of its own reforms.

Labour's latter-day leveller, Mr Tony Benn, does not agree

that we have a free press, however. 'We live in a society', he declares, 'where the right to free speech has been taken away', since the media use their power to support the *status quo* and to distort and conceal alternative points of view. Leaving aside the supposed malice of the media, what Mr Benn is complaining of fundamenatally is the absence of any *right* to be published – a right very different from that of free speech, and one which has never in fact existed in any media. Everyone has the right to hand out pamphlets of his own making, to write letters to editors and make speeches to anyone who will listen; even to start his own newspaper if he can raise the funds. Otherwise there is no alternative to persuading the existing media that what he has to say is worth reporting for its own sake. There are times when one wonders if Mr Benn is not arguing for the printing and broadcasting of everything, unedited, and for minority views to be treated as if they were majority views.

Nevertheless, there is enough in what Mr Benn says about the tendency of the media to stay with the *status quo* to win as hearty a 'hear-hear' from radical people as the bishop must win from more conventional folk. It is true, I think, that there is not enough *variety* of newspapers and networks. The problem is how to increase their number without diminishing their ability to survive economically. Indeed, the most immediate problem is how even the existing number can survive.

The freedom of the mass media to carry on as they are is also threatened in the world forum. The twentieth general conference of UNESCO narrowly managed to ward off a Declaration of Principles, widely supported by communist and Third World delegations, which would have given governments an internationally recognised right to control the reporting of their affairs in the media of other countries. It sprang from the resentment, not entirely unjustified, felt by such governments at finding themselves reported abroad by western reporters who do not share Third World or communist values.

The case for controls was defined in terms of 'strengthening peace' and 'combating war propaganda and racism', terms which it is hard to oppose. But the draft Declaration added that all such reporting should be done 'with due respect for the sovereignty and legislation of the countries in which these media are located', and that 'The mass media should make known the versions of facts presented by states, institutions and individuals who consider that the information published about them has done serious harm to their efforts' to strengthen peace, fight war, racism and colonialism. What was more, it was to be the duty of governments to 'ensure that the mass media coming directly under their jurisdiction act in conformity with the present Declaration', which would seem to be a limitless invitation for governments to turn foreign correspondents into official noticeboards.

The classic case for this sort of control is that world news services are dominated by wealthy western nations which are accustomed to the luxury of individual dissent and criticism which developing states cannot afford. Moreover, it is argued (rather more speciously) since liberationist governments represent the people, for a foreign reporter to criticise the government is tantamount to criticising the people, which is a hostile and inadmissible act.

Most western reporters would readily grant that Westminster–Washington democracy is not necessarily applicable to Asia, Africa or even Yugoslavia. But they know enough about human nature wherever it may be, and under no matter what political philosophy, to be certain that no government can represent everybody nor can it long resist tyranny and corruption if it is immune from criticism. Certainly western reporters should try harder to understand why Third World rulers feel they must act as they do: but it would be counter to the Christian view of man to accept that a party machine can be immune to sin, or that a dissident individual does not matter.

I would not pretend that our human interest tabloid papers are written by teams of concerned Christians; nevertheless the Christian tradition that not a sparrow falls without our heavenly Father caring, and that even the hairs of our head are numbered, lies behind the obsessive concern with individual cases which dominates the western media. If we were to adopt the People's Democratic style of emphasising collective achievement, state policy speeches, and individuals only as symbols,

7

then we might escape the charge of media triviality, but I doubt if our media would come any closer to the kingdom of heaven.

It is far from easy in these days which have seen the London *Times* closed down and the BBC blacked out by trade disputes to talk of the media in the same breath as things of the spirit. Far from easy and yet I think it has to be done, as indeed it should be done with many other trades and occupations from medicine to street sweeping. For there *is* a moral issue; and although morals are by no means the whole of religion, a religious person cannot think of one without the other. I should like to go back now to the Bishop of Southwark's complaint, so that I may begin this study of the moral dilemmas of journalism with some very specific cases. Just what can have upset him?

I made the experiment of taking a month at random* and making of its new bulletins and front pages the very worst I could – compiling the very sort of catalogue of woe that would make the Bishop switch off.

Day 1. In New York, a man nicknamed 'Son of Sam' pleads guilty to six murders committed, he claims, on the instructions of his demonically possessed dog. A broken oil tanker, the *Eleni V* drifts along the coast of East Anglia polluting the beaches as she goes.

Day 2. In Rome, the body of the kidnapped ex-premier Aldo Moro is dumped by the Red Brigade terrorists. In London, much is made of the dismissal of a trainee chef at Claridges for improperly seasoning his ratatouille. At the Old Bailey, five people are found guilty of running a sex agency and accepting credit cards for services rendered.

Day 3. Princess Margaret's divorce application is announced. The Queen and the Archbishop of Canterbury have no comment to make, but a Mr Roddy Llewellyn says he will never wed the Princess.

Day 4. The press spot a new partner for Lord Snowdon. The National Society for the Prevention of Cruelty to Children report that an average of two children a week are killed by parental brutality.

* 8 May – 8 June, 1978.

8

Day 6. 'Has the Princess made divorce respectable?' asks the *Sunday Times*.

Day 7. The media describe how two 'killer boys' or 'mini murderers' humiliated and scared to death an 84 year-old Wolverhampton widow who had recently discharged herself from a geriatric hospital. Six children from a single Essex village are killed in a minibus crash. The media carry interviews with shocked parents, and stunned teachers.

Day 8. MPs now 'calling for' the usual 'full inquiry' into the case of the killer kiddies. The boys, aged 4 and 6, are back at school, allegedly boasting of their exploit. ITN interviews one of the mothers and shows an identifiable shot of her son.

Day 9. Scores of whites reported massacred in southern Zaire. Charlie Chaplin's coffin and corpse are recovered in Switzerland where two men had been holding the remains for ransom. Less prominently reported, 50 Africans are 'killed in crossfire' during an attack by Rhodesian Security Forces. A 19 year-old police constable is murdered in Worksop.

Day 10. A Merseyside husband seeks an injunction to stop his wife having an abortion. Plans to rescue the surviving whites from Kolwezi, Zaire. The latest about a Yorkshire Jack-the-Ripper who is believed to have murdered eight prostitutes.

Day 11. French paratroops storm Kolwezi.

Day 12. Fleet Street provides its own headlines with printers' strikes and threats of closure.

Day 13. Hideous reports of butchery in Kolwezi. Only occasional acknowledgments that blacks as well as whites died.

Day 14. Still more about Kolwezi and 'Son of Sam'.

Day 15. Kolwezi again. King Hussein is marrying wife number four.

Day 16. Princess Margaret gets her divorce. The anti-abortion husband loses his case and his child. From Kolwezi it begins to emerge that by no means all the liberated inhabitants love President Mobutu or the French.

Day 17. Lady journalist loses case to get a drink at El Vino's 'men only' bar in Fleet Street.

Day 18. Revelation that a Blackburn clergyman has had a sex

9

change operation thus (it is said) breaching the Church of England's rule against women priests.

Day 19. Sensation over teacher's claim that an 8 year-old Manchester girl is listed as available for debauchery in a California directory.

Day 20. Prince Michael of Kent plans to marry a Roman Catholic baroness whose marriage has been annulled. In Germany, the U.S. Army has to pay £8,000 compensation to a lady interpreter improperly dismissed for failing to wear a brassiere.

Day 21. Much speculation about the impact on the constitution of Prince Michael's plans. Man throws bottle at Prince Charles, photographers get smashing shot.

Day 22. Elderly British couple murdered in France.

Day 23. Birthday Honours List.

Day 24. Mr Jeremy Thorpe MP interviewed by police about supposed plot to kill a former acquaintance, confessed homosexual Norman Scott.

Day 25. Having lost to Peru, the pride of Scotland's football team admits to taking drug before playing in the World Cup. An Arab sheikh buys twelve thousand special bricks in Britain and spend two pounds per brick air-freighting them.

Day 26. 17 year-old wife admits alleged rape was really voluntary. Argument over whether Greater London Council is right in contemplating 'ghetto' estates for Bengalis.

Day 27. Government minister describes parliamentary broadcasting as 'a public relations disaster'.

Day 28. Guy the gorilla of London Zoo dies. Press Council declares London paper's account of a rape incident to have been 'inaccurate and sensationalised'; warns papers to report such events in grave and sober terms not calculated to titillate, and to avoid giving clues to victim's identity.

Now it would not be surprising if you deduced from all this that the Bishop was right, and that the mass media were exclusively concerned with what was either violent, racist, voyeuristic or trivial. I have even made one or two striking omissions, such as the nude photographs of the American girl who jumped bail while on a charge of kidnapping a Mormon missionary.

But the diary I have presented above is, in fact, an incomplete one. It is deliberately slanted to support the critics' case. I have taken pains to omit most of the more significant front page stories of the period. You will find nothing here about politics or economics, nothing about human rights, refugees, wars, other than the Kolwezi operation, nothing about the Middle East, Indo-China, the Soviet Union or Japan, not because the media failed to report them (they did not so fail) but because I wanted to make the point that such a caricature of the mass media – a caricature which many critics mistake for the truth – is not accurate. The items I have listed may be the ones that catch your eye, but perhaps your eye should take some of the blame for that, or perhaps you should take a different newspaper or tune to a different station. For such items do not in fact make up the bulk of the papers and news programmes.

Yet it is not my purpose by any means to argue that the media are perfect and blameless. I have many complaints to make of them, though they are not always the ones the critics would like to have endorsed. Let me go back over my catalogue of woe and see how much or how little of it can be justified, even in its distorted perspective. For I do not believe it is even as black as I have made it seem at first sight.

You could argue, for a start, that the gruesome 'Son of Sam' murder story earned its space only because it appeals to the conviction of most British people that the streets of New York are crawling with psychopathic killers. Such a prejudice does exist, and no good is done pandering to it. It can hardly be argued that the British have a right to see American justice done, or need to be warned as citizens and taxpayers. On the other hand the story of the leaking oil tanker, though it appealed to the public taste for disaster, did also respond to a genuine public concern. It warned people along the east coast of what might be coming their way and it supplied the entire nation with facts on which to base its opinion of what needs to be done about the problems of shipping traffic and oil pollution. It also raised some doubts about the competence of the authorities dealing with the disaster.

If 'Son of Sam' can only be justified in terms of our ancient hankering to have our blood curdled (and that goes back to the age of wandering minstrelsy), the tragedy of Aldo Moro is a good deal easier to justify as of public interest. Terrorism is now international and we need to be warned so that we can take our own precautions. Furthermore for Christians martyrdom of this sort and the redemptive quality of unmerited suffering have a special significance. Was it in good taste for newspapers to show the body, curled up in the boot of a car? I doubt if the term applies: it was a pathetic but powerful image that will not easily be forgotten.

The affair of Princess Margaret and Lord Snowdon might have raised more serious doubts about motives and values. And yet, given the fact that we have a royal family which we require to live on a pedestal, it seems to me the matter was handled with surprisingly little nosiness and a good deal of sympathy. The royal press officers handled their side of things with considerable dignity, the Church forbore to moralise: it was not so much that the Princess had made divorce respectable as that the public had already developed a tolerance to divorce, even among princesses.

The matter of the 'mini murderers' is, to my mind, the nastiest on the list; not just in itself (it is sickening to imagine in the mind's eye), but in the shallowness with which it was reported in some cases and the superficiality of the reactions it brought out. When such events are reported there is almost a race among public figures to be the first to 'call for a full inquiry' (no one ever asks for a simple 'inquiry'), and curiously this is treated by the media as if it were significant news. Some of the comments made on this particular occasion barely stopped short of demanding that the children involved be exterminated or sentenced to transportation. None of them showed much interest in comprehending what sort of conditions could produce children, or parents, like these.

I shall argue strongly in the pages that follow for the right of the mass media to find out and publish what the people need to know – which is often much more than those in authority would *like* them to know. And it is often possible to argue convincingly that the exposure of one case of abuse will alert the public to the existence of others. Reporters know all too well that one example of baby-bashing or one attack by an Alsatian dog seem to bring to light a whole string of others. And with luck something is done to curb the menace, thanks to the media. But reporters also have reason to believe that a hard core of such cases is always there, lying unnoticed below the surface, and will probably remain long after the fuss has subsided. The reporters may for a time continue to report them, but when editors lose interest on the grounds that they are no longer news, reporters may as well save their pencil lead and turn elsewhere. There is a strand of nasty little horrors – maimings, batterings, bullyings and depravity – running through life that neither exposure nor neglect by the media will ever destroy.

In a case like the Wolverhampton murder I am always left wondering, 'But what really happened? What were the *real* facts? How much more is there to know, if only the reporter had the time and co-operation and his editor the space to tell it? It cannot be *that* black and white. Perhaps the local people do have a need to know. Indeed one can be pretty sure they know anyway, including the names and addresses involved. But who benefits from this nation-wide publicity? Did anybody at all?'

And again, after the Essex minibus accident, did it benefit anybody, beyond the boundaries of that particular village, to see the headmaster of the school being coaxed into saying how he had told the other children of their companions' death, and how they had taken it? Yet one has to be very careful of trying to lay down hard and fast rules about such matters. Interviews with the bereaved are not always the heartless, impertinent affairs you might suppose. People often *want* to talk about their loss or outrage. It could have been, though I have not heard that it was so in this instance, that a parent or teacher had the urge to protest about the lack of safety precautions on schools outings. I have been in precisely that situation myself, when a daughter of mine barely escaped with her life from a fire during a winter sports expedition to Italy. It appeared to me, from her account, that the fire precautions had been inadequate and I was glad to tell the media about it in the hope that something would be done to protect other children.

13

Again, the father of a young Salvation Army teacher from Northern Ireland shot by guerrillas in Rhodesia was interviewed shortly afterwards by Anne McNamara of the BBC *Sunday* programme. What he had to say about his lack of bitterness and his faith in God's will must have uplifted thousands. What may look like an intrusion into private grief may turn into a breaking out of it. I am not saying it is always so, or that every attempt at an interview should be pressed home and printed.

But what about the massacre and rescue of the white community in Kolwezi? Richard Dowden, writing afterwards in the *Catholic Herald*, remarked, 'It was simply "Wild Black Men Kill White Men, Rape their Women and Murder their Children". All Fleet Street's underlying racism was disclosed ... great human drama at the airport, lots of eyewitness accounts of gory details, brave white soldiers coming to the rescue. Did I miss it, or did a newspaper or radio or television news programme ever actually relate what was going on?'

Certainly it is ironic that, within the same month, there were two cases in Rhodesia of large numbers of African villagers being 'killed in crossfire' between the security forces and the guerrillas. One social acquaintance of mine used to attack me roundly when we met, on the grounds that the BBC, under communist influence (he maintained), always played up incidents like these and never mentioned what the Africans were doing to the Europeans, or 'only very pianissimo', as he put it. Things were different that month, at least. The media's coverage of Kolwezi was never less than fortissimo.

How far were attitudes prejudiced by race? Prejudiced is a harsh word. Conditioned might be fairer. To expect the mass media to give equal prominence to *all* mass killings would be to demand they report very little else, or none at all. And to demand that they carry a complete account of what was going on is to ask the impossible in a very precarious situation. I doubt if it was possible for anyone to find out, in a hurry. And it would probably have needed a convinced pacifist as editor to resist the general feeling that here was an exciting military adventure. There simply are not many pacifist editors.

To my mind the real failure of most of the media in southern Zaire, with the possible exception of the *Observer* and the *Financial Times*, was their failure to have taught the public long ago that here was a corrupt, incompetent and unpopular regime that was heading for disaster.

The Mersyside abortion case, sandwiched in the middle of the Zaire adventure, unquestionably raised some important legal and moral questions. The Roman Catholic Archbishop of Liverpool was moved to make a sermon of it a few days later. And here again there was no question of the parties concerned being intruded upon against their wills. They both had propaganda to make and they seized their opportunities to make it, issuing press statements, granting interviews and posing for photographs without inhibitions.

The Yorkshire Ripper's doings may perhaps have excited the bloodthirsty, but any of his later victims should have been warned by the publicity, and that publicity should play its part in helping to catch him. The police have clearly sought it by supplying reporters with information and identity pictures.

The sex change vicar, poor fellow, reads to me like a story in which a certain amount of giggling and nudging has been disguised as serious theological concern. Quite apart from the fact that the man dutifully resigned his ministry months earlier and made no attempt to embarrass the church he loved, it is surely sophistry to argue that the case had any real relevance to the ordination of women. Once more, who can possibly be said to benefit from the publicity? The unfortunate ex-priest? The Church? The general public?

As for the 8 year-old girl in the porn directory: here was an instance of a third party – neither a parent nor a journalist – airing an incomplete story in public, which might have done a great deal of harm. For it soon emerged, as the following day's papers recorded, that the child had been entered on the list innocently and accidentally. It was a case in which everybody would have done better to take longer checking their facts.

Prince Michael's plans for a mixed marriage seem to me no more – perhaps no less – interesting than those of anyone else so remote from the throne. At best, they were another sign of the times, for better or worse, in the marriage field. Yet they were of some ecclesiastical significance to those who are concerned with Roman Catholic doctrine on annulment and relations with other faiths. As with Princess Margaret's divorce, there were official spokesmen available who co-operated with newsmen constructively and with dignity, and the couple themselves even held news conferences.

Mr Jeremy Thorpe's interview with the police might just be described as his own private affair. But the whole business had always been one about which reporters believed they knew more than the law would allow them to print; for which reason they kept it on the simmer for months until such time as the law itself took the lid off.

As for the rest, it is probably as well to remember that, for example, not every allegation of rape is true and not every football team a pack of supermen. The minor war that broke out between the sporting press and the Scottish national football team at the 1978 World Cup was, I suggest, not the result of too much exposure to reporters but too little. It might have been avoided by greater openness, instead of hiding the team away and leaving the media to feed on rumours and guesses. As for Sheikhs, gorillas and brassieres, they may not be of any great moral or political significance, but they help to make the world's woes somewhat less oppressive and even to put them in perspective.

Perspective is something to keep in mind throughout any discussion of the supposed sensationalism, prurience or triviality of the media. My month's anthology is without any context but its own. It completely lacks the great slabs of routine sport, parliamentary and business reporting, let alone the advertising, that normally soften the blows.

Nor is it true that the press and broadcasting are only interested in *bad* news. I shall return to this later, but editors in my experience are hungry for *good* news and would always prefer to put something cheerful and encouraging in their headlines if only they knew where to find it. It is hard to know how to measure the goodness or badness of news, but my own rough efforts suggest that the average front page or ten-minute news

16

bulletin is about 40% bad, 30% good and 30% neutral. A good deal depends on your social and political philosophy.

It is quite possible that having leant too far in one direction to begin with, I am now leaning too far the opposite way. I should hardly have a book to write if I thought there was nothing wrong at all with the media. It should be evident from what I have already said that I believe the media do too often pander to people's lowest common appetites, that in some cases they tell too much to too many and in others too little to most. The charge of 'trivialising' makes me hesitate because what may seem trivial to somebody inside a situation may seem a most expressive symbol of it to the outsider (the reporter) who is trying to enlist the imagination and understanding of his readers. What does worry me is the persistent *superficiality* of our journalism; not merely the lack of penetration into the background of the story, the 'why did it happen? what does it mean?'; but still more the speed with which we skate over the very facts of the event, seldom pausing long enough to make sure of what really happened in the first place, what the context was.

I regret to say that broadcasting is particularly prone to this, and partly for technological reasons. A story may break at one o'clock, be analysed at ten-past-one, reacted to at five-fifteen, raised in the House of Commons at six and projected into the future at ten – and all before one is really certain what took place to begin with.

At least a newspaperman has, generally speaking, only one deadline a day, that is one point on the clock by which his report must reach his editor's desk. Broadcasters, however, have an almost continuous rolling deadline; there is probably a bulletin every hour that he should try to reach, and major news programmes at intervals of five hours or less. Modern electronic communications make it possible for him to supply these demands with something, but it may be something short of the full story which he has little time to unearth. I do not say it is wholly impossible for him to do an adequate job; some reporters are more energetic and incisive than others, but a good deal is bound to escape enquiry. And it is my belief that the speed

17

with which broadcasting can mop up a story between midday and midnight discourages newspapers from taking up the same story more thoroughly themselves. To someone who has heard it at lunchtime on Monday, it is no longer news at breakfast on Tuesday. Thus the really thorough job may never get done at all. The media can be robbed of authority by their own speed.

The same technology is partly responsible for one of the aspects of the media's activities that worry me most: their tendency, as I see it, to overstretch the public's concern and sympathy. I am not saying that a drought in central Africa, a refugee exodus from Burma, does not matter. Thanks to the mass media, we care more about these disasters today and do more to alleviate them than we ever did fifty years ago. But at the same time our concern about them tends to be restless, volatile, leaping from one end of the world to the other, arriving always too late and leaving usually too soon. The result, as readers, listeners and viewers have confessed to me, is that the public is at first caught up in a wave of helpless sorrow, then directed towards charitable relief which is not always well-directed or received and is usually too late, and eventually declines into a feeling that no matter how hard one tries it doesn't seem to do much good. Relief organisations like Oxfam and Christian Aid are very well aware of these dangers. They would much rather emphasise their work as agents of steady, unspectacular development work, not as occasional fire brigades. But the mass media have trapped them, in the public imagination, in the fire brigade role. I shall have more to say about this later, but I have already indicated how the media themselves have been trapped by technology into this kind of coverage.

I shall also be trying to explain how the media have fallen victims to the peculiar economics of their industries. For technology has made it possible for us to have a service of information that we can hardly afford to pay for. And having whetted their appetites, that same technology has made it possible for the public to have glimpses of truth which are so truncated as to be misleading and even dangerous. This is especially true of television. It is possible, at vast expense, to transmit film or even live events from, say, Buenos Aires to London, instantly. And it is natural enough for people to believe that when they have seen the picture on their living-room screen, they have witnessed the event, that they know what happened. But nobody who does not understand the situation from within knows their full meaning. That is why the pictures themselves are not enough. That is why there is a commentator speaking over the pictures and explaining them, and a great deal more depends upon him than is usually granted. Does *he* understand what is going on? Does he have the time and experience? Do the pictures give him a chance to be heard properly? I have my doubts. And I have further doubts – even making allowances for my prejudice as a practitioner of the written and spoken word rather than of the moving image – about the effect that television has by diverting vast sums of money away from media which are well-suited to the carrying of information to one which is rather poorly-suited for the purpose. In short, while more and more people are coming to rely on television for their news, I think it is a poor news medium.

It will also emerge from the following pages that while I am, indeed, concerned about the shortcomings of our journalism in this society, I am also concerned (paradoxically, you may think) that journalism should not be taken too seriously. In fact I believe, as a result of some thirty years' experience, that the influence of the mass media has been grossly over-rated – very largely as the result of a desperate search for somebody or something to blame for our current woes. The media themselves have to share the blame for this misconception: we take ourselves too seriously.

We take ourselves too seriously at the highest professional level. Being a journalist, it has been said, is a fascinating profession because you meet such interesting journalists. It is an extremely incestuous occupation. Newspapermen spend a great deal of time reading each others' newspapers, broadcasters listening to or viewing each others' broadcasts. If you wish to communicate with the public, it is of no use trying to address yourself directly to it, even if you could visualise so shapeless a creature. Your labours are in vain unless you can

19

first get your piece past that Cerberus of the air or page, the chief sub or editor of the day. He is the man you are writing for, and as the result of years of adaptation to their circumstances he and his mates have arrived at a house style and a set of news standards which allow very little room for eccentricity or non-conformity. It would, in fact, be very difficult for them to get through their work on time if they stepped outside that framework.

Once again, we are up against the pressures of speed. But what I am more concerned with here is the informal news consensus that dominates the media; the unhappiness everyone feels if they are not saying the same thing. It has never seemed to me in the least surprising that, since God chose to create men in many varieties and many different situations, we should find ourselves a world of many varied nations, religions, languages and churches. The real oddity is that anyone should imagine we ought to be uniform. And yet, in the world of the mass media, there is a strange hankering for uniformity.

It is popularly supposed that every paper would like to have its own exclusive scoop every morning, and its own front page looking totally different from everybody else's. Nothing is further from the truth. The occasional scoop is gratifying, but only so long as everyone else endorses it by picking it up in their next edition. Nobody likes to be out on a limb for long, with a story that no other paper will touch. What seems to make editors happiest is to spread out all the morning's papers and broadcast transcripts on the office floor and to find that they all have the same stories in roughly the same order and with no contradictions.

The true philosophy of Fleet Street is not cut-throat competition but solidarity. Defensively you might say that only reflects reliability. If everyone is agreed, the chances are their collective view is the correct one. But if, as I personally believe, the truth is more complicated than most people think and can never be seen from a single point of view, then a uniform picture is likely to be an incomplete picture of what actually happened.

Complexity is essential to most truths. Unfortunately it is an enemy to straightforward communication. Ever since the popu-

20

lar penny press took information out of the hands of an educated elite and made it the right of every literate human being, it has been an axiom of mass communication that good journalism is simple journalism, easily understood by anybody. Up to a certain point that is not a bad objective. A journalist who is simply talking to himself is useless. But not everything can be conveyed to everybody – at least, not without falsification. Nor does everybody need to know everything.

But if there is one thing I can usefully attempt in this book, on behalf of those who are likely to read it, it is to explain what journalists are trying to do, and why, and what obstacles lie in their path. I have no intention whatever to lecture or reprove my colleagues. One important fact that the Christian reader should bear in mind is this: that the majority of newsmen, readers and listeners today are *not* committed Christians. That is no condemnation of journalism, though it may be a criticism of the churches which have failed to reach the sort of people, lively, intelligent and often deeply concerned people, who become journalists. The churches, whose very mission is to communicate, are woefully ignorant of the media of mass communication which could put them in touch with the world they are commanded to evangelise.

I should not want it to be thought that I see a distinction between journalism and Christian journalism. Christian journalism is only *true* journalism, just as (in Hans Küng's words) one becomes a true human being by being a Christian. A Christian newspaper like the *Church Times* would be a liability to the church if it did not pursue the basic principles of all journalism. Christianity may affect, and *should* affect, a paper's choice of subjects and its editorial comments. It will very likely affect the motives of its staff in working for it and its readers in buying it. But no one will get plus-points in heaven for being a *Christian* journalist or even a *good* Christian journalist, any more than the good Christian will get into heaven any faster than the plain good man. We are Christians as an expression of what we are, not because Christianity provides us with a set of magic spells with which to achieve success.

2. Vile Scribblers

Prodnose: I detect that you are going to be evasive. I put to you the following: that the mass media are sensational, lurid, lascivious, cynical and biased; that they are subversive of morality, patriotism and due respect for authority; that they pander to the lowest common mentality, personalise issues of principle, trivialise what is serious, seek out whatever is negative, ignore what is positive, violate the privacy of the distressed, prejudice the course of justice, glorify the criminal, instil violence in the young, neglect the law-abiding, bribe the weak-willed and generally falsify the record.

Priestland: Yes, I think that's a reasonably unfair statement of the case. I don't doubt most of those vices are practised from time to time. But given the British distrust of what they fear to be highbrow education (a distrust not entirely undeserved) and given the economics of the media, you are actually getting a pretty high standard for your money. It is about the only alternative to having the media run as a state social service or subsidised by the Arts Council, and you wouldn't like that, would you? Anyway, if you dislike the media so much, why do you buy their wares?

Prodnose: I don't read those frightful papers. I read the *Daily Telegraph* ...

Priestland: Quite right, it has much the juiciest coverage. But why are you so worried about papers you wouldn't touch with a barge-pole?

Prodnose: I have other people's morals to consider. I care about them, if you don't. Besides, you can't have it both ways, saying journalism is a sacred trust and yet that its perversions don't matter.

Priestland: Do I contradict myself? Very well then, I contradict myself. You are bound to when discussing anything in the round. In any case, I am not saying journalism is faultless. I am saying that its really important defects are mostly ones you haven't named, to do with distracting us from the really important things of life that are under our noses; to do with communication and understanding and the glory of God ...

Prodnose: Oh, sophistry!

Priestland: No, honesty. Shall we proceed with the book?

The trade of journalism has never, in England been regarded as a respectable one. Reporters are addressed as 'Gentlemen of the Press' in the vain hope they will behave as such, rather than as a statement of fact. As a result, many capable journalists escape, if they can, into public relations, the academic world or Parliament – this last giving the lie to the theory that there is real power to be had in Fleet Street.

Things are otherwise in the United States, where a reporter might just quit his paper to become a Professor of Communications (for journalism is regarded as worthy of serious study there), but has been known to turn down the offer of a seat in the Senate with some scorn. The Washington correspondent knows that he has an honoured place in the nation's capital: just after Senators, in fact, but well ahead of members of the Lower House. In Washington the Press Corps are addressed as 'Gentlemen' with sincerity, and for the most part they deserve it. Not only have they inherited the German tradition of scholarly journalism, deeply researched and written in somewhat tedious detail at times, but the American media also have a constitutional role to play in the working of the nation, a role that is neither established nor regarded as necessary in Britain.

I shall be turning to the journalist's role as a bridge-builder in my next chapter. For the present my object is to raise the low esteem in which the British hold him, by explaining something of his task and its limitations. For while that task is, at its best, far nobler than most people realise, the limitations are also far more severe.

Most people (an easy phrase, but I think it applies here) regard the approach of a journalist with deep misgivings. They are afraid they are going to be bullied, have words put in their mouths, be misquoted or made to look foolish. Once, in exasperation, I told the representative body of a certain church that it was 'as timid as church mice about using the media'. One of its members wrote to me later, saying timidity was too simple a diagnosis. 'We are uneasy', he wrote, 'about the way in which broadcasting and the press take material and shape it to their own style of presentation. We are no longer in control of our own material. This is a real difficulty, because we have no effective concept of presentation. William Temple once summed up the issue very neatly with the comment that the trouble with a certain famous interviewer was that he wanted the right answers to the wrong questions – which is what one does feel when one is the raw material.'

All of which both sides should take to heart. Reporters and interviewers because they do tend, in their mad stampede to beat the deadline, to forget that their subjects are real live people who exist beyond the story in hand, and are not just temporary sources of information: and the public, because it illustrates the unnecessary helplessness people often feel when confronted with the media. There is no real reason why anyone should feel at a disadvantage when confronted with a reporter. After all, *you* have the information *he* needs. Yet people act as if there were a great gulf fixed. Part of the trouble is, I suspect, the bizarre diction that sometimes transforms the story on the printed page. BISHOP BLASTS NUDE CHOIR OUTING probably started off with a suffragan saying he thought the choirboys of St Prunes' should have taken their bathing trunks with them to Margate.

Again, there seems to be a conviction that the mass media are somehow responsible for creating the disasters they report: that the world would be a better place if there were no reporters at all. This may not be entirely rational, but the instinct is very deep and I have heard it vehemently expressed in many forms during lectures and discussions. Even governments succumb to it, accusing the media of being responsible for every kind of disaster from violence in the streets, civil war in Northern Ireland and poor sales of British cars, to the decline of sterling on the foreign exchange markets. The precedents for blaming

24

the messenger for the bad news he brings are very ancient, and well summed up in the journalist's favourite play *Anthony and Cleopatra*:

Act I, Scene 2, Messenger: The nature of bad news infects the teller.

Act II, Scene 5, Cleopatra: Thou shalt be whipp'd with wire and stew'd in brine, Smarting in ling'ring pickle.

Messenger: Gracious madam, I that do bring the news made not the match.

Cleopatra: Though it be honest, it is never good To bring bad news.

Putting myself on the other side of the stage, so to speak, I can see the modern Cleopatra's point of view. News is by definition that which is new, what has changed. And if there is one thing that hard-working middle-aged, middle-class people feel they can do without, it is more changes: technology has speeded things up beyond our emotional and physical capacity to adjust to them. And yet here come the media, heaping more and more changes on our heads every day. It was, I think, a former Director General of the BBC who remarked that since only the young had the stamina to work in television and only the elderly the time to watch it, TV was tending to become the young telling the old what the old would rather not hear: the generation gap in vision.

Allied with this is the suspicion that the media would really like to run the country and are constantly trying to undermine responsible authority. In Britain, there is no doubt about it that journalism does attract somewhat more than its fair share of left-wing young people – or at any rate, young people who are not card-carrying conservatives (though the same is not so true higher up). These are the probing, challenging types that good journalism needs, and like most British leftists they mature with experience.

25

In the United States, President Lyndon Johnson firmly believed that it was the mass media that led to the failure of his war effort in Vietnam and ultimately obliged him to renounce a further term in the White House. This, he insisted, was sheer irresponsibility. The press did not know what he knew about the war. Indeed, he was the *only* person who knew *all* about it and so was qualified to take the decisions about it. Richard Nixon had much the same convictions about the press. Both presidents, one from Texas, the other from California, believed themselves to be the victims of smart Jewish intellectual journalists from New York and the east coast, snobs who thought they owned Washington and despised those who did not share their education.

Both presidents certainly had a strong personal flavour which did not suit every palate. I remember hearing Lyndon Johnson compare Sir Harold Wilson to 'a blind hog rooting in a dung heap'. But I am convinced, from my own time in the White House Press Corps, that it was not snobbery that turned reporters against them, nor what eventually turned them out of the White House. The more time passes, the more the facts pile up against Johnson and Nixon. The press and broadcasting were right, not prejudiced. The war in Vietnam was always a disaster from the start, and Nixon's abuse of his presidential powers was deep and disgraceful. A Christian correspondent of any human sensitivity, was bound at some time or other to ponder whether it was right for the media to destroy the careers of these two leaders. But in view of the power and authority which a president commands, including the power to send men to their death by the thousand, it was not an unequal match in favour of the media. I don't see how such correspondents could do other than they did.

But, as I suggested, the role of the media in Washington is rather different from that in London. The American Constitution guarantees the freedom of the press, and the 'Right to Know' law grants anyone (not just journalists) access to a very wide range of official files. There is a separation of powers in the American system which makes it difficult for Government and Congress to monitor each other's activities and communicate with each other day by day. Ministers do not sit in Congress ready to answer questions or initiate legislation. There are no great focal debates in which the issues of the day are hammered out. The head of government, the President, who is also head of state cannot rise to make a statement at short notice. The system is in many ways defective and full of gaps and it is up to the media to fill those gaps. The media are, in fact, essential to the running of Washington and to its communications with the fifty sovereign states of the Union. So the American media are not so much rivals to the establishment as part of it.

The British Constitution (which does not even exist on paper) makes no such provision. With all due respect to the Great Reform Bill of 1832, which I was brought up to regard as a close second to Magna Carta, Britain is still governed from day to day by a modified form of the feudal old boys' network, of which the working journalist is not an acknowledged part. Even under a Labour government, there is a certain class element in this. As I say, journalists are not gentlemen; and this feeling is even stronger among the wealthier, better educated readers. Some of the sauciest headlines of the day are to be found in the *Daily Telegraph* (for example, SEETHROUGH NIGHTIES STOP MILKMAN'S VASECTOMY or SEX-IS-FOR-FUN ATTITUDE THREAT TO MARRIAGE), but readers like my friend Prodnose are full of indignation that vulgar, popular rags are prying into matters which the 'quality' press can be trusted to handle more discreetly – and in greater detail. Lurking in the background is a class-conscious regret that literacy has got into the wrong hands.

The Established Church gets drawn into this. The American dollar bill asserts *In God We Trust* and there is a staunchly patriotic strain in much American preaching. But it was an essential part of American revolutionary doctrine that there should be no single established denomination linked with the state and claiming to speak for it. Britain, on the other hand, still has an Established Church, and there remains a lingering assumption that through the pulpit it is responsible for rallying national morality – not the press. One has only to read through the small print of the 1662 Prayer Book to see what a powerful

27

moulder of opinion the Church of England has been. With Sunday attendance at first compulsory and then conventional, with its prayers for the preservation of the political and religious hierarchies, and its social and economic assumptions, it is not surprising that those in authority came to regard the Established Church as the moral cement binding the nation together. The great columnists and editorialists of this medium of communication were the bishops and the clergy.

Victorian newspapers acknowledged that leadership, for they were written largely for upper-middle-class Anglican readers. The rot set in as education ceased to be the monopoly of that class and moved down into the commercial and industrial classes. Newspapers became popular and nonconformist. They were no longer the private notice-boards of the privileged, but instruments of education, investigation and reform. Increasingly they broke away from the Established Church, fell into the hands of dissenters and became rivals of the pulpit, subversive of the traditional order. And this usurpation of the moral leadership of the nation by the media has never been forgiven. Now that the House of Bishops has itself become reforming and progressive – the majority of them are far from conservative about race, human rights or the neutron bomb – the feeling becomes all the stronger that moral and political examples should be set by the Palace of Westminster, not Broadcasting House or Printing House Square.

Authority likes to have leadership concentrated in one place. It prefers to have bishops discussing the morality of abortion from their seats in the House of Lords, for there they are safely integrated into the system and under control. Authority does not like the church or the mass media to behave as if they were leaders of opinion *outside* the established framework.

But *do* the media lead opinion? I have very grave doubts whether they do. I believe, and this is surely in keeping with the Christian doctrine of free will, that people are a great deal less malleable than they are thought to be. Loud alarms are often raised that this or that bias in the media is subtly driving the public to right or left. What I find most disturbing is the intolerance, in what is supposed to be a liberal democracy, of views that readers or listeners don't happen to share. Complainers will always assure you that *they* are not affected by such rubbish – they are only concerned about its effect on people of lesser intelligence, particularly young people. The young people usually turn out not to have been listening anyway. My own impression is that the public in general has a heavy keel of scepticism that prevents it being blown off course by passing squalls. Certainly I have never had the experience of meeting a listener or reader who complained he had been tricked by the media into voting the wrong way. But I have met plenty who were convinced that other, less perceptive, voters had been so deceived.

Most newspapers make a clear distinction between their news and their views, and editorials are notoriously the least read part of the paper. Broadcasting systems in Britain do not have editorials at all. Interestingly, American radio stations are urged and expected to editorialise on the grounds that failing to do so is cheating the public of a service and shirking a journalistic duty. But an American station is also expected to give equal time to the other side, and I am bound to say, for myself, that I am glad British networks are kept out of this business. It is hard to say which does more damage to good broadcasting: nailing partisan colours to the mast and alienating half the audience, or turning the studio into a debating chamber and cancelling out every 'You're a liar' with 'You're another'. Better, surely, to follow the unspectacular path of informing, informing, informing and resisting the temptation either to endorse or condemn.

I believe that is the proper path for any journalist who is dedicated to the best values of democratic Atlantic society, rather than to those of eastern Europe. I also believe it is one specially marked out for the Christian.

What I have said should be highly acceptable to those, usually non-Marxists, who insist that the job of the journalist is to 'stick to the facts'. The trouble is, the same people often complain that the media have become altogether too permissive, too ready to substitute a generalised wishy-washy tolerance for austere moral judgment. They are quite prepared to let

29

journalists go beyond the facts, provided it is in the right direction.

The beginning of a Christian understanding of journalism is that the truth is very much more than the obvious facts, and that even those are not so easily come by. I call this a Christian understanding because I believe it reflects the approach of Jesus himself. Throughout the New Testament we find him slow to rush to the obvious conclusion, or to condemn, and painstaking in listening to other people's points of view. He constantly rejected stereotypes, making friends of publicans and sinners, even taking seriously a centurion of the occupying forces and resisting easy, vote-catching lines of appeal.

The basis of all journalism is finding out and recording the answers to the classic questionnaire 'Who, what, when, where?', and, if possible, 'How and why?' Simply answering those first four questions can be a great deal more difficult than you might imagine. The last two are often impenetrable, though they are the most important. Much of the time, the reporter is trying to describe an event that he did not himself witness. He was not actually there when the car crashed, the baby fell from the window or the trade union leader told the Chancellor what he could do with his wages policy. The reporter has to reconstruct events on the basis of other people's accounts of them, and those accounts may be influenced, even distorted, by anything from self-justification to carelessness. You may have played the game in which an unexpected happening is staged in front of a group which is then asked to write down what happened. No two accounts are quite the same. A reporter is supposed to be trained to ask the right questions and check the facts. But how can he publish the truth when those who know it can't or won't tell it?

Trade unionists often complain about poor reporting of industrial disputes, but the reporter who turns up at a strike-bound factory may find the greatest difficulty in getting either side to talk to him. Management are afraid of exacerbating the situation; rank and file union members are forbidden to talk to the press and point all enquirers towards the nearest shop-steward. The lack of openness is frequently blamed on past

30

betrayal by the press. But without openness the reporter can only get a partial picture.

He is lucky, too, if he is given time and space to present it. For the reporter is always under pressure. To some extent he loves it. Journalists may grumble about stress, but (to quote an old professional quip) the bars of Fleet Street are full of newspapermen suffering from stress deprivation.

Editors naturally want to get all the work out of their men that they can. But added to this is something like an industrial hysteria, generated by a mixture of competition and convention. Newsrooms go through different phases and fashions. In some the reporter or specialist correspondent is king and the editors and sub-editors dance fairly closely to his tune. But in others, the organiser at the desk takes over and imposes his view of the world and how it should be reported on the men who are actually out there coming to grips with it. I am talking here about something more than the news consensus. I refer to a sense of proportion, shape, style, direction. This is perhaps more noticeable in broadcasting than it is in the world of newspapers. To a certain extent the placing and headlining of newspaper items does govern the reader's attention. But if he wishes to wander off the front page into the byways of page 2 or 7 or 13, no editor can prevent him doing so. The reader can totally ignore the front page and turn immediately to the sports page. But in a broadcast bulletin the listener cannot get to items 2, 6 or 8 without sitting through numbers 1, 3, 4, 5 and 7. He cannot break away from the conducted tour. And there is a further stylistic peculiarity of broadcasting, especially of television.

A newspaper is a newspaper. It is all more or less journalism. It is not a play, a comic novel or a school textbook. But a television network is probably all these things as well as being an audio-visual newspaper, and being closely related to the cinema (from which it derives most of its style), show-business values have inevitably leaked through into the journalism. If news programmes were not entertainingly presented by reasonably attractive people, they would seem amateur and out of place. No television news organisation is prepared to say, 'We admit our settings are bleak and our newsreaders ugly, but what they are saying is more important than how they look.'

Perhaps the worst treason is that too many able journalists who enter television allow themselves to be seduced by its technology. They become so anxious to demonstrate their mastery of it that their basic newspaper standards of what is important become overgrown with clever technique. It has happened to me in my time. The medium takes over from the message.

Except when it is being blatantly didactic, television is a poor medium for delivering detailed messages. It is, on the other hand, unequalled for delivering the big emotional punch – joy, horror, sympathy. It can convince people who have never been east of Norwich that Cambodia exists and is populated with real live dying people. But *why* they are dying, only the commentator can explain, and too often the pictures are beckoning us away from what he is saying. And in television, as in radio, once the words are spoken they are gone for ever. You cannot go back and read them again in your own time.

Taken with the dependence on pictures, this actually slows down the pace at which television can deliver its information (or it should – some news programmes are like high-speed firework displays, leaving not a rack behind). Television has to be simple and concrete. Radio, without the pictures to worry about, can get a good deal more information into the time and even attempt a few abstract ideas.

I begin to suspect that the more information people receive, the more they find reason for doubts. The great ages of certainty and faith were also ages of ignorance for most people. When information is not only plentiful but blurred by speed, people become confused by it. Is one doing them a Christian service by adding to the confusion, or (almost as dangerous) by trying to bring order out of chaos by overlooking threequarters of the facts? Yet news programmes are staples of broadcasting. It is not just the appeal of 'see and hear it now'. The raw material of news is given free; the broadcaster has only to process, present and transmit it. To fill the same period with fiction would be much more difficult.

I wrote earlier of how competition and convention spurred the editor on. One convention is that old news – say, older than 24 hours – is no news. If newspapers had only rival papers to worry about, this could hardly be justified on grounds of competition, for few people, apart from newspaperman themselves, bother to compare one paper with another, or regard it as a great disaster if their paper misses a story. The real competition is with broadcasting. Newspapers do their best to keep pressing forward in the wake of the swifter medium, and the broadcasters in turn will comb the papers to make sure there is nothing they have missed. Thus the mysterious spirit I have named the news consensus is formed, identifiable but shifting, for it does not hang about waiting for people to catch up. Anyone who separates from it to pursue his own hunches at his own pace soon begins to feel uneasy and isolated and to imagine his readers or listeners drifting away to follow the pack. The consensus feeds upon itself. A journalist is also likely to feel uncomfortable if not only his reporting but his *interpretation* of events is markedly different from that of his colleagues in other organisations.

This is nothing so obvious as editorial policy or bias. Most newspapers (as opposed to broadcasting systems) have a committed editorial policy of some kind. They may be aligned with a political party, they may be for or against the Common Market or Communism, and this will obviously and fairly frankly affect their leading articles and choice of emphasis. Most readers are well aware of this and hardly need protection against it. They stay with their papers because they feel at home with them. There are even papers – I would say the *Sun* was one of them – which are virtually *anti*-newspapers, deliberately leaning away from the more mind-taxing events of the day and towards what is relaxing and entertaining. For millions of housewives and commuters, such papers help to remove the unpleasant taste left in the mouth by the early morning newscast. I can see little harm in this, indeed it may even be a service to mental health.

Britain has an undeniably free press, though there is no guarantee it will remain so since some of those who would like to

33

raise its standards seem to think the best way of doing so is by compulsion. But I have suggested that ours is a generally conforming press. There is usually little disagreement, after a day or two, over whether a budget is a success or a failure and whether a speech is to be labelled 'tough' or 'conciliatory'. Many speeches are, in fact, both – which is awkward. For journalists have come to expect a story to have a consistent point, almost a plot, with a beginning, middle and end and a sharp cutting edge – where possible, with blood on it. The best story, one that is clearly understandable, has what is known in the trade as 'a good, hard lead': a sentence or two saying that something has *happened* and who, what, when, where. Very often (whatever the conventional wisdom) it is possible to write the story in two or three different ways, emphasising different aspects with equal validity. But chief sub-editors tend to be very unhappy if *their* leads are not endorsed by other chief sub-editors' leads. Nor are they keen on fancy writing.

Lest this begins to sound like an old reporter's complaint about the crassness of the men on the desk (a war as old as that between cat and dog), I hasten to add that fancy, even literary, writing can be wholly out of place in a news bulletin or an agency dispatch. It can get in the way of the information, draw more attention to the writer than the story and look as inappropriate as a rose-bush in a potato patch. Read out loud, it can sound ridiculous and trip up the newsreader.

Some kind of simple, direct style is not unreasonable. The danger is that, under pressure from the consensus, it may lapse into a fashionable dialect of journalese. Journalese itself is understandable. Much of it is spread by the news agencies, pumping their pithy paragraphs into every newsroom in the nation. Reporters come rushing in to catch their deadlines, and to save time and argument slip into the jargon. It takes a senior correspondent with much prestige behind him to break out of it, if he has not already become its slave.

If every paper and newscast sees itself as competing with, or rather, keeping up with, every other newscast and paper, so is every story competing with every other story. It begins by competing for a place in the page or programme at all, for on a reasonable day most editors have far more material to hand than they will ever use. They would be alarmed if they had not, for they hate to feel they are scraping the barrel.

The reporter or writer is anxious to get his material before the public. If he does not, he does not exist. So he will present his story not only as clearly and accurately as he can, but as attractively and as eye-catchingly, even to the point of bringing in words that stress its importance, like *crisis, drama, threat*, perhaps even pushing the event a little further than its protagonists realised they were going. I once received a handout from the Church of England proclaiming, 'History will be made when a West Indian steel band plays in the garden of Westminster Abbey . . .' History?

But the fact is, every reporter and handout writer is doing much the same. And so the front page or news bulletin ends up with the winners, as it were, of the hot news heats; every item just a little heightened, signposted, simplified – especially the marginal items that might not otherwise have been accepted. The journalist knows that with intense pressure upon space or time, his story stands a better chance the shorter it is. No ordinary citizen ever believes he has said a word too many. He is shocked to find his painstaking explanations, so carefully adjusted, hacked down to a few stark assertions.

Have I been describing a dishonest profession? Journalists do not see it that way. Indeed, the Code of Professional Ethics of the National Union of Journalists is an exacting one. Yet I know, from personal experience, what it is to be the victim of hasty reporting. Once, when the rest of the BBC had been knocked off the air by a power failure, I found myself having to *ad lib* to camera for the best part of an hour from the only studio that was left in operation. Next morning, a newspaper I had not even spoken to carried a breathless interview in which I was quoted as saying I had not even expected to be on the air that night . . . odd, since I was billed in the *Radio Times*. When I protested, I was told, 'Well, old boy, it was the sort of thing we knew you'd have said. Didn't do you any harm, did it?' I am sure the fact was that a reporter had been under pressure to produce some human interest – fast.

This taking of short cuts usually comes from the best of motives. It is an attempt to widen the readers' interest and sympathy, to make things easier for him. The fact that you have taken the trouble to pick up this book suggests that *you* may not need such help. But what about those whose education is less advanced (Britain is, I suspect, a country that does not really believe in education), and who, given the choice between the *Sun* and the *Times* would think you were crazy to ask? A better question might be, isn't an editor wasting his time even trying to interest the great British public in, say, an American presidential election? And yet we are agreed that our voters *should* be widely informed, *should* be encouraged to look upwards and outwards occasionally. Over-simplification, sensationalism, is part of the price we have to pay for efforts to do that.

If you have already reached the conclusion that the media of mass communication are past redemption, the next question might be whether the conscientious Christian should become a journalist or broadcaster at all. Perhaps he should accept the Muggeridge line rather earlier than Malcolm himself did, and get out – or work only for *Third Way, Crusade* or *Christian World*. But that, I think, would be defeatist and arrogant. There is no need for a journalist to stay with a paper or network which he believes to be corrupting. But he should have a certain respect for the tastes of ordinary people, even if they do not coincide with his own.

Here I am not endorsing the slogan, 'Give the people what they want' – the fact is, people do not know what they want until they see what they can have, which may be something they would never have dreamed of left to themselves. The Christian journalist, for example, ought to be able to show that what is good and virtuous and true is as attractive and intelligible as what is evil, corrupt and false. He has every reason to try harder, to excel in his craft.

But, to be realistic, he is no more likely to transform his paper or his network than he is to alter the whole town where he lives – that is, unless he becomes editor or mayor. What is needed, surely, is not that Christians should eschew popular journalism, but that they should become deeply involved in it as journalists, audience and news sources – sources that co-operate with journalists frankly, openly, even lovingly when information is sought. And, as they do so, they should try to appreciate the difficulties the journalist is up against and the limitations on what the individual journalist can achieve.

It is equally important for concerned readers and listeners to appreciate the limitations on what the editor, the journalist's boss, can do. For a start, his paper has got to pay its way somehow. A high-minded paper that goes bankrupt is a futile gesture. Even a public service broadcasting network must be able to demonstrate that it is serving an audience of reasonable size for the money it is getting. Yet even the readerships of the *Times* and the *Guardian* are not enough to support their papers unaided. Indeed, the higher quality the paper the *more* likely it is to be dependent upon some form of subsidy, either from a sister paper of more popular appeal or from advertising, from printing supplements, or some other fringe activity.

All over Fleet Street at the moment, there are balance sheets in the red. The industry is the victim of its own earlier success. The fact that Britain is a small, centralised country enabled the national press to build up huge circulations during the first half of the century – circulations which advertisers came to expect when placing their material. Confronted now by competition for advertising from commercial television, papers are desperate to maintain high circulation figures. They have paid their printers sometimes twice as much as their journalists, to persuade them not to disrupt production; they have held back new and more economical printing technology which would have cost the men jobs; and, as a result, Fleet Street has become a dinosaur park. The rising costs of paper, communications and every other supply have made it almost impossible for the press, and to some extent broadcasting, to give the public the service it has come, extravagantly, to expect. To make even a middle quality paper independent of high advertising revenue, one would probably have to double its price; but put the price up, and circulation falls. The fact is, the public, especially a high-minded public, cannot afford to pay for the truth. It is already getting more than it pays for.

The future, I suspect, lies in the further development of local papers and broadcasting, reinforced by syndicated columns and services. There will be some drawbacks to this; for example I cannot see that a local paper or station will care even as much as Fleet Street about the Third World or the arts. But it may also be less susceptible to industrial hysteria and the news consensus, less inclined to get its audience unprofitably worked up about events that don't really concern them, and more inclined to feature things they can actually influence.

I think this should be as good for journalists as it will be for the public. London journalism today is in a somewhat unhealthy situation, for it has attracted an army of bright, active, able young people with not enough creative, constructive work to do. They do not have an acknowledged constitutional function; Westminster and Whitehall rather resent them and the organisations for which they work are often frustratingly big so it is hard to make much impact in them or on them. But in a smaller, local news organisation the journalist can visibly serve his community, see the results of his work, meet the people for whom he is working. In Christian terms, the pastoral responsibilities of his ministry become very much clearer. And as ordained Christian ministers are already finding all over Britain, a local radio station is a worthy vehicle for the gospel.

It seems to me that despite its shortcomings and its failures, its blemishes and disgraces, journalism is a calling for the Christian. Surely there can be few more honourable or worthwhile professions than that of trying to find out the truth – the how and why as well as the who, what, when and where – and to pass it on, clearly and responsibly to the public. It also seems to me to be a valid service to supply some entertainment at the same time. For I think we have to accept that people read newspapers, watch or listen to broadcasts, not only to be informed, educated and improved, but to be cheered up or delivered from the tedium of commuting or waiting in the doctor's surgery (perhaps it would be better to cultivate stillness – but that is not in most people's background). Every news item has some element of entertainment in it; that is why journalists call their work 'stories'. It is impossibly austere to insist that there should never be anything trivial, scandalous or thrilling in the news.

In honest journalism it goes without saying that clarity and accuracy should go hand in hand. But that is not always so easy to achieve. The inner truth of a situation is often extremely complex – as the early councils of the church discovered when they attempted to define the Trinity. On a more everyday level, events in Africa usually take place against a background of tribal loyalties. You can scarcely understand the workings of the various black groupings in Zimbabwe (Rhodesia) without this background, and yet it is seldom given because the names are outlandish, the implications strange, and it would only clutter up the narrative.

And so the news we get is often over-simplified in the cause of clarity, and thus it becomes inaccurate. It is profoundly disturbing. But until we become a much better educated society there is no easy way out of this dilemma.

3. Builder of Bridges

The year 1978 has been well described as 'The Year of the Three Popes' – Paul VI and John Paul I and II. As Religious Affairs Correspondent it is not surprising I spent a good deal of it in Rome, watching anxiously for ambiguous puffs of smoke from the chimney of the Sistine Chapel, and trying to persuade tight-lipped cardinals to reveal what had been going on in the Conclave. Seeing they were upon oath to keep silence, under pain of excommunication, they were reluctant to talk about anything much beyond the air conditioning and the food. Papal conclaves will surely be the last institutions upon earth to adopt the sort of openness every reporter longs for.

This particular reporter longed for either of the John Pauls to carry openness into at least the most obvious place for it, the Vatican Press Office, an institution whose impenetrable prose and plain lack of information make it the despair of all condemned to make use of it. For the point of my introducing a Roman note here is to illustrate how there *is* a demand for news of a spiritual nature, if only the churches are willing to supply it. Through papal funerals, elections and coronations, I and my colleagues from all over the world were astonished at the enthusiasm of our far-away editors and, beyond them, the watching and listening public. And the Popes themselves, I believe, sensed this and were ready to lean out over their protective courtiers to reach that public. They had good news to give, and the world longed to hear it.

Both of the John Pauls held audiences for the press in the first few days of their reigns. I shall remember John Paul II sturdily shaking hands all the way up the Sala delle Benedizione and pausing to exchange greetings in half a dozen languages. But still more I shall remember John Paul I, that humble and humorous man, gently lecturing us on our responsibilities, breaking away from his turgid Vatican script to insert illustrations. He did not hesitate to tell us where we had gone wrong, for he had read some of our articles about the pre-conclave manoeuvres and really, he insisted, it had not been like that at all – no lobbying or pressure groups.

Still he insisted that ours was a noble and exacting profession. He had heard it said that St Paul himself would be a journalist if he returned to earth. And surely not just a reporter. John Paul thought he would be at least a director of Reuters, or call round at Italian TV to ask for time on the air – or maybe from NBC.

But the trouble with journalism these days, said the Pope, was that it became too easily absorbed in trivialities – not what Napoleon III actually said to the German Emperor, but what colour socks they wore and whether they were smoking. The Pope begged us, if we ever had to handle his poor efforts, would we please be merciful and understanding and concentrate on their more significant aspects?

Impossible to deny to so pleasant a man, or to his successor. One can only hope that John Paul II will eventually be able to break through the walls of the Sala Stampa and let in the light – to realise the link between his own role and that of the journalist, even beyond their common 'ministry of the word'. For the priestly caste of ancient Rome took the title Pontifex or Bridge-maker, the builder of bridges between gods and men, and that title passed on to the Popes. The journalist in his more modest way also builds bridges, between man and man. There is no reason why he should not build them between man and the church, if only the church is not too haughty and suspicious to use them.

But the prejudice dies hard. It is uphill work to try to remove the establishment suspicion that journalists are irresponsible, encouraging if not actually causing half the troubles of the world they report on. It is a world of which everyone, including the Pope, is much more aware than they used to be; a global village as McLuhan puts it in which everyone knows the gossip and recognises the chieftains, priests and witchdoctors from five thousand miles away. The sheer scale of the news, the range of what we can know is itself terrifying.

This is one reason why the colour of Napoleon's socks is a rather soothing and human piece of knowledge to have, though I doubt whether any reporter would use it as more than embellishment to a more substantial dispatch. I think, however, that journalists may be presenting a heightened, simplified, symbolic and in many ways unreal news world, and that it is very hard to avoid doing so. Unless they are to embed the relatively small number of events that are actually new and striking within a great mass of what is everyday, humdrum and rather boring, journalists can never present a completely accurate model of the life we all lead. But to create such a model is not our purpose, and I do not think many people would buy one if we made it. Few people would have the time to read their way through it. And so we select. We are bound to select and we are expected to select.

The main function of the journalist, and especially the reporter, is to carry selected messages to and fro, building bridges across which people may reach out and understand one another. I have already argued that journalists are usually far too busy performing this task *ad hoc* from day to day to plan and execute any grand design of influencing the course of history. Indeed, I have a fairly low estimate of how influential we are. If I valued my work in terms of the results it had achieved, the warnings heeded, follies avoided, charity shown and violence restrained, as a result of my thirty years' hard labour at the typewriter and microphone, then I would have given up long ago. The bridge-building and message-carrying are something to be pursued almost for their own sake, like pure scientific research; and like scientific research, to be justified as service to the truth rather than to expediency. This is not to say we should prostitute our immortal souls by failing to count the consequences of what we do. It seems to me, however, that it is not what we journalists write that alters the world. What really matters is what has happened, and journalists play very little part in making it happen.

The mass media did not make Lenin happen, or Hitler,

42

Nasser, Churchill or Mao Tse-tung. Nor did they invent communism, nazism, the IRA or the colonial liberation movements. Indeed, although they reported all these developments in the end, the mass media managed to sleep through the formative years of most of them. Go back in history to the days before there were any mass media, and you will find just as many vices, fads and follies sweeping the world as in our own communicative days, though perhaps they sweep a little faster now.

It would be stupid to pretend that journalism was entirely isolated from the way the world goes. Yet, although at times it may be a distorting mirror, I do not believe it reflects what is not already there. The circulation of causes and effects is far too complex to be seen as a flow in one direction. Influences feed back and forth into each other, modifying each other constantly. Yes, the behaviour of a terrorist gang may be affected by media publicity; but it is dangerously naïve to conclude that 'They only do it for the publicity – stop that and you'll stop the terror.' There is much more to mugging, rape and Pakkibashing than an idea taken from a newspaper.

To concentrate on the media's responsibility is to oversimplify people and the way they acquire their motivations. People may recognise their views, clearly articulated, in the media; but they acquire them from many sources. Some very deeply felt opinions about Jews, blacks, Catholics, homosexuals and 'long-haired layabouts' are never expressed in the media at all, or only to be abhorred in the editorial columns.

For people do much more than read newspapers, listen to the radio and watch television. They talk to each other, occasionally write letters, constantly observe what goes on around them and interpret it in the light of their education and upbringing. The influence of friends, relatives, workmates, teachers and pastors, the arguments and conversations of daily life and the surroundings of home and workplace are of greater influence than the mass media. And of all the media of mass communication – though the one least identified as being in need of control – surely books have proved to be in the long run by far the most influential. From the Bible and the Koran to the works of Augustine, Aquinas, Luther, Calvin, Rousseau, Darwin, Clausewitz, Nietzsche, Marx, Freud, Jung, Keynes and even Dr Spock – the evidence is literally voluminous. In comparison with authors, neither journalists nor anyone else should over-rate the influence of journalists.

We are, I submit, better fitted to the humbler role of bridge-builder or message-bearer. But we must always pause to ask, bridges between what? Messages between whom?

Not long ago there was a campaign by the Anti Nazi League to deny to the National Front the free party political broadcast to which the Front felt entitled as a result of its past electoral showing. It was debatable whether the Front really *was* entitled to it, since the allocations had always been made by informal agreement among the established parties. Nevertheless the Anti Nazi League took the possibility extremely seriously, arguing that freedom of speech is not unlimited and that as non-believers in liberal democracy, Front members were not entitled to avail themselves of democratic freedoms.

The moral dilemma here is a difficult one to escape from. On the one hand, a long-established right of free speech and fair play for all comers; on the other, a group which does not practice either, but wants to take advantage of both for its own purposes.

What should the stand of a Christian journalist be? It does not follow obviously that there is a specifically Christian line to take. I would expect to find good Christians on both sides, some arguing that judging not and loving one's enemy must include putting him on the air, others retorting that failure to resist evil in every possible way is in itself an evil. Christianity is no insurance against party divisions.

Legalistically there is a strong case for tolerating anything that is not *prima facie* illegal, at least until there is reasonable ground for supposing the law is about to be broken. And there are laws enough on the statute books to prevent almost anything that might cause pain to the police. On the other hand Quakers, for their part, have always recognised the right, even duty, to defy the law for conscience' sake, provided one is ready to take the consequences.

It seems to me that the issue must be resolved on other grounds than 'The law says this' or 'Jesus says that'. As an individual journalist, responsible before God for what I do even above my editor and my union, I think I can find my way by trying to discern what God has meant me to be. In my case he has made me an English middle-class, liberal-democrat Quaker Christian, and such I have accepted. I can only choose the course of action that is authentic for me by comparing the options open to me with this accepted heritage. Am I the sort of person who would do this for this reason, or that for that reason?

For myself, I should not want to be the sort of person who would help a spokesman for the National Front – or any other party – to violate the law of love *and* the law of the land by insulting members of other races and inciting the public to violence against them. But in such cases there is really no difficulty. One would simply not report such a speech, and I think it highly unlikely that any British editor would in fact require one to do so.

But what if the words spoken were restrained and within the law? Then I would not wish, either, to define myself as the sort of person who prevented others from making up their minds about them. To assume that role seems to me arrogant and sinister. It is to assert 'I know best. I know what might subvert the judgment of others less intelligent than me.' And it is to assert also an extremely dangerous precedent. Who or what is to be forbidden next? Christian pacifism, perhaps. To argue that one should never allow anything to be broadcast that might put a fascist in a good light seems to me both to overrate the appeal of fascism and underrate the ability of a healthy democracy (for Britain is not Weimar) to argue it down. But my underlying conviction is that listening to others, attempting to understand them, and responding to them (George Fox would say 'answering that of God in them') is the only alternative to writing them off as beasts and coming to blows with them, which is blasphemous.

45

I said I had over-simplified in describing the journalist as a bridge-builder or message-carrier without further qualification. As I have indicated above, he would not wish to allow himself to be used as a vehicle for what is obviously illegal or corrupt. He will hardly – if he is a Christian – communicate messages that are malicious, obscene, cruel or patently false. So the journalist, if he accepts responsibility for the consequences of what he does, must be involved in *processing* the messages he carries. Indeed, that is what the public pays him to do.

Frequently you meet people who insist that the journalist should 'stick to the facts' – though often it is precisely the facts that are in doubt. What the speaker often means is 'stick to the official version of the facts', or in journalistic terms 'just print the handout'.

There was a time when much news broadcasting consisted of little else. Any interpretation that might be added in a lower paragraph had to be carefully balanced so as to indicate that on the one hand there were those who considered the official view to be the correct one, while on the other there were those who felt it left something to be desired. The *Times* also used an elaborate code of obliquities. Unless he was an expert cryptographer, the reader was liable to leave the story little the wiser for what he had read.

Now, there are indeed times when even the most expert correspondent is uncertain of the rights and wrongs of the story. In particular, he does well to avoid forecasts and prophecies such as who the next Pope will be, when the Prime Minister will call the next elections and what the rate of inflation will be doing in six months' time. The longer one stays in the news business, the more inscrutable it becomes. But it would be very odd indeed if an experienced specialist did not, after some time, develop his own wisdom and his own sources of information enabling him to check and evaluate the official handouts. He will be able to say, 'The government claims that inflation is down to four per cent, but their figures have left out the cost of housing,' or 'The new Ambassador to Madrid is Mr Frederick Muffin – who does not speak a word of Spanish and has never been farther afield than the Isle of Man.' He has certainly altered the message here, but in doing so he has made himself a more reliable messenger, and given his readers the benefit of wisdom he has been accumulating, at their expense, over the years.

I believe the public today does expect journalists to evaluate the messages they are given, to sort out those which are not worth delivering and rewrite those which are too long or too hard to understand. There is a place for the newspaper of record – the one that carries the full text of the Queen's Speech or a reasonably full account of an important legal judgment. But no newspaper, and certainly no broadcast, has room for all the information unloaded on it, and no reader or listener would think he was getting value for money if it were all passed on without further digestion.

The messages carried by the journalist are delivered, at one end of his bridge, to that amorphous addressee the public. But at the other they come from very distinct individuals, from politicians, civil servants, villains and heroes of all kinds. And it is here that the journalist is in the most delicate and responsible position, a position to make, break or tarnish a reputation, arouse anger or anguish, and in extreme cases expose his subject to hatred, ridicule or contempt. For such are the possibilities of the interview.

Yet for the most part there are no such dramas involved, and for every injustice complained of there are thousands of routine exchanges that satisfy everyone concerned. Most interviews are a matter of one person who wants information asking another who has it, and getting it. Ah, but *why* does he want it, and what is he going to do with it? For some reason – possibly the films, novels and plays written by failed journalists – there is a stereotyped image of the sensation-seeking, tough-guy reporter with his foot in the door and his cheque-book at the ready, hunting in packs with flash-bulbs popping and press-tickets in hatbands. In fact, it is hardly ever like that – where it is, the performance is not always unwelcome to the celebrities involved.

For the most part, reporters are as civilised and house-trained as the people they are sent to interview (occasionally more so). Treat them kindly, tell them the truth and they will usually respond as one ordinary human being to another. It is even possible to say 'No, I have nothing I want to tell you and I must ask you to leave', and the chances are they will go. Another approach is to remember the times you have been happy enough to read of or watch other people being interviewed, and to follow suit. It is very seldom that reporters are out to 'expose' you unfavourably. What have you got to hide? Reporters have nothing to gain by getting things wrong; but they cannot get them right unless the people who know the facts will tell them.

Myself, I am surprised how docile and co-operative most people are with reporters, and how seldom they refuse or complain. It may not make life any easier for me and my colleagues, but I feel bound to point out that while I would prefer everyone to be frank and open, there is nothing to prevent them saying, 'I'm not interested in answering that question', or 'I think that's a stupid question', or (as the late Clement Attlee occasionally did), 'I hear you – what was your next question?' You can even insist on switching off the tape recorder and starting all over again. Such behaviour may not make you the reporter's favourite assignment, but there is still no reason why you should abjectly surrender your judgment to somebody else, simply because he works for a newspaper or radio station.

None of which I need to tell to the average interview victim, who is usually a professional politician, union leader or other public figure. In such cases it is often hard to tell who is the victim – the public figure or the reporter who is being employed as the message-carrier. Such victims come to the slaughter willingly and with alacrity, they are certainly not compelled to come and quite often they are paid. Listeners who complain about the toughness of interviewing would be surprised if they could hear the conversations that go on in the studio before and after the recordings. Once I was about to interview a certain English bishop when he leant across the table and urged 'Go for me! Go for me! I'm much better when people really attack me!' So I did, and when it was over the bishop clapped his hands and cried 'Splendid! I think that brought out the best in me.' I'm glad I was able to quote him when his angry defenders wrote in. Politicians are even more likely to put on an act for an interview, and their highly developed technique of talking without answering the question ('I'm glad you asked that – but first, if I may, I'd like to make this absolutely clear . . .') invites some fairly tough counter-measures from the interviewer who is trying to check and clarify the message.

And yet I have to say I am constantly, uneasily aware of the shortcomings of the interview, especially as a broadcasting technique. Too often, I think, its dramatic qualities (two voices are more entertaining than one) obscure the absence of any real content. Lacking the time and resources to investigate a story in depth, it is tempting for an editor to think he has covered it by playing a quick interview. Yet there is seldom much to be gained from hearing a professional interviewer sparring with a professional interviewee – and a good deal of time to be lost. I do not doubt the value of questioning public figures, provided the questioning is done in private and then used as part of the reporter's general stock of knowledge. Done in public it encourages two things: the circumlocutions and evasions I have already mentioned, and the actual forcing of views out of season. One might, for example, ask a Prime Minister where he stood on abortion and extract an admission that he was opposed to it. This might well produce the headline, 'Prime Minister Opposes Abortion', which could produce a party crisis – a crisis which had not been there before, because abortion had not been a lively issue and would never have become one had not the interview precipitated it. There is, I am afraid, this constant risk of the interview interfering with the normal course of events, and I think it is one which the conscientious journalist should always keep before him. Is that question really necessary? Will it extract an answer of any real value, or will it force an issue before its time?

If a journalist's job is not only to carry messages but to clarify them he will have to devote special attention to those messages which are unpopular, or come from unpopular people: the kind of messages that are easily dismissed as propaganda. The outrageous speeches of President Amin, the latest editorial in *Pravda* or ultimatum from a strike committee are usually tossed into the waste-bin as insincere, meaningless rubbish. At best they are turned inside out as concealing more sinister motives. But the fact is, language means *something*: presidents, editors and union leaders seldom employ it to make nonsense noises, and though its meaning may turn out to be other than we would have liked ourselves, maybe we should seriously try to understand what it is. For if we believe that *all* men are the children of God, it is surely blasphemous not to take them all seriously or to assume that only 'our side' is worthy of consideration.

This means that in building bridges with, say, the Soviet Union, one has to take seriously the constant insistence upon peace-loving and try to understand how this can be squared with the maintenance of vast armies. In building bridges with the trade unions, one has to penetrate why a handful of men can feel justified in bringing an entire industry to a halt. And in building bridges with black Africa, one has to explain why, for example, both Amin and Kenyatta purged their countries of Indian traders. This is not popular work. On different occasions it will probably be described as anti-semitic, racist, fascist, communist work. But if people are left without such understanding of each other, they can only hate each other. We do not have to support or approve of each other's ideologies, but we should appreciate that the other side is not either sub-human or crazy.

In Broadcasting House, London it says *Nation Shall Speak Peace Unto Nation*. Race unto Race, it might have added. Surely there is no nobler work for the Christian journalist than that of racial and international understanding. Here is the hardest work of all, and in some ways the mass media are working against themselves. Consciously, most of them labour for peace and harmony, but at the same time the information they supply of the behaviour of other races, other nations encourages subconscious hostility.

The very nature of news as 'that which has changed' militates against acceptance and understanding. I sincerely believe that one of the first duties of the media is to serve as a public early warning system, to warn of danger and abnormalities. But what this brings on to the front pages is a succession of violent or sinister episodes, and often there is very little explanation why

50

they have happened. Probably there is no room, possibly there is little interest either. And, as they might have said, good news is no news. The normal and harmonious we should expect anyway.

Thus we do not hear about the hard work, self-sufficiency and obedience to British law of Asian immigrant families; nor have we heard much about India's miraculous achievement in feeding a population that has almost doubled in thirty years, and in achieving a trade surplus. To most British people, the United States is a nation of drugs and violence and materialism, rather than the painting, musical and literary powerhouse of the west. Nor do many people care to recognise the social and economic progress being made in the Irish Republic.

Here, too, are bridges to be built. How is it to be done?

To some degree, foreign reporting is like any other reporting: there are facts to be gathered, checked and clarified and then passed on. But traditionally (and I regret the fading of this tradition) the Foreign Correspondent has been a rather special figure, even a romantic one. To envious colleagues at home, he appears to spend his life in the sunshine, idly reading *l'Osservatore Romano* in one of the cafés on the Conciliazione with a glass of Punt e Mes at his wrist. Well, it *does* have its romantic moments; actually to be paid for living in Paris, Madrid or Rome is something for which the correspondent is devoutly grateful – though it is usually a privilege he has earned and not stumbled upon by luck. But it is also a life of some hardship and occasional danger, even if the correspondent is ill-advised to keep telling this to his colleagues back home. He does occasionally get shot at, arrested, beaten up and bullied. The hours he works are so wildly anti-social no well-organised trade unionist would look at them. The strain on his family is considerable and he is often separated from his wife and children for weeks at a time. And especially if he is a broadcaster – a very large amount of his time is taken up not with journalism but sheer communications: shipping film, waiting for overdue radio circuits, endlessly dialling London for an intelligible, crackle-free line.

When I speak of the foreign correspondent, I have in mind the classic correspondent who lives in the foreign capital, has a

51

home there and keeps his family with him; for he can learn an enormous amount about a foreign country through the friends and activities of his wife and children, especially if the children go to school there. British broadcasting has an excellent record still of appointing this kind of correspondent – expensive though he is to maintain. Fleet Street, alas, has seen the number of its resident foreign correspondents, especially for the populars, steadily decline. Instead, thanks to the jetliner, we have the 'fire-brigade correspondent' (also favoured for television assignments), who will go anywhere and cover almost anything – whether or not he speaks the language. There are techniques for coping in these situations, and we have all used them: the dash for the Reuter's office, the quick briefing at the British Embassy and drinks with a local English-speaking journalist. But they are really no substitute for the man who lives there, knows the history and the personalities involved and their long, illuminating background.

Such a man has to be both prophet and missionary – and he has to love the country and the people, or he would do better to leave. This does not mean, at all, that he has to side with the government in power. But if he is the kind of man who fumes with rage against 'these people and this bloody place' he is likely to prove a very bad bridge-builder, and his messages will be jaundiced.

The good foreign correspondent, it seems to me, has to try to speak *for* the country he is covering, explaining to his home audience *why* its peoples are behaving as they are, trying to justify their beliefs. In this sense the correspondent is a missionary for them. But he must also have insights into the meaning of their life, and be able to project those insights homeward. And in that sense he has a prophetic role, a kind of poetic role. He has to communicate *what it is like*, so that his audience can begin to feel if for themselves. And a part of what they will feel, one hopes, is the brotherhood of man, stemming from the fatherhood of God. Without this, our interest drifts towards a kind of voyeurism, as at a freak-show or peepshow, 'See the funny foreigners and their curious habits'.

I have been personally concerned for some years over how to

bring about better reporting of what is loosely called the Third World, here in the First. In the Second, the communist world, the solution is simple: an order from above can unloose a torrent of tedious handouts on a defenceless but earnest public. But you can't do that in the west, where readers are historically sceptical of government, have not been conditioned to regard a steel works as a miracle, and have a low threshhold of boredom.

Looking back over the years it is hard to deny the Third World claim that the west shows interest in the developing countries only when there are wars like Biafra, Katanga and Vietnam, disasters like Bangladesh, Ethiopia and – where were those earthquakes? – or figures of controversy like Indira Gandhi, Idi Amin and the Emperor Bokassa. Then the fire-brigade hurries in, usually too late, lives off the abnormal until it begins to heal, and then hurries out again, not to return until the next crisis.

The impression this gives to the western audience is of a Third World which is incompetent and uncivilised and whose inhabitants lead lives of poverty, superstition and oppression. It is rather as if the United Kingdom were reported in terms of nothing but strikes and the IRA.

The harm this has done is manifold. The new nations of Asia and Africa need all the sympathy and self-confidence they can get if they are to stand on their own feet and not to fall into the arms of worse masters than the ones they have quite recently parted with. When they see and hear their failures displayed by the western media, this only convinces them of western malice and drives them towards those who are ready to be more sympathetic. It encourages censorship and further self-deception, it leads to the expulsion of western correspondents and the out-break of futile international press wars. The Third World starts to complain that western news agencies have a monopoly of international news traffic, and schemes are drawn up for non-aligned agencies which are little more than exchanges of self-serving government propaganda. It has to be said that the touchiness and paranoia of some Third World governments – understandable though it may be – does more harm than good to the cause of communication.

Paradoxically, the disaster-seeking approach to foreign news can give the correspondent his one chance to say something positive about the country concerned. I once covered a drought in Maharashtra which enabled me to say something about the endurance of the local people and the resourcefulness of their state government which would never otherwise have reached the air. But that same disaster brought fury to the central government of India which once again had to undergo the humiliation of seeing pictures of starving Indian children all over the world's press, followed by a bombardment of charity offers. The international relief organisations, like Christian Aid, Caritas, Oxfam, were trapped: they had long ago reached the conclusion that what was needed was steady development aid, but they knew that what brought the money rolling in was the urgent disaster appeal and pictures of starving babies. And yet again there was the risk that sooner or later people would turn away from the collection box groaning 'Not *another* Indian disaster!'

What is needed is a continuous service of sympathetic but reliable news about the Third World in sickness *and* in health, for richer *as well as* for poorer, so that when there is a crisis people will not only appreciate the background but will also see it in the perspective of what is normal. But how can one get this sort of reporting of the unspectacular, when space and time go only to the spectacular? For a start, it has to be well written by correspondents who are interested in the people they are covering and determined to communicate that interest. They need to be assured their work will get a hearing, and this means setting aside space and time on a regular basis and not just when there is a crisis. It means a regular Letter from Here or Column from There.

Which is all very fine, but how is it to be paid for? Partly, I suggest, by tax concessions which would make it cheaper for news organisations to maintain resident correspondents abroad; and partly by cheaper tariffs for international press communications. There must also be a far greater tolerance of critical reporting. I have argued that western reporters need to be more understanding of Third World efforts and susceptibilities; but the Third World needs to return the compliment by understanding that western reporters are not representatives of their governments, that they make a traditional distinction between a country and its government (to be anti-Gandhi is *not* the same as to be anti-Indian) and that a western reporter who uncritically sends back everything he is given is not likely to be believed by his audience at home. Above all, the Third World needs to take the western media rather less seriously than it does. A country that opens itself up to visitors and allows the chips to fall where they may is far more likely to win affection and respect than one that permits guided tours only and monitors every word that the foreign media send back.

Ideally a reporter should be a fly on the wall, unheeded but seeing everything. The more he is personally drawn into the proceedings, complained about, swatted at, the more antagonistic he is likely to become and the more his work will be coloured by feelings of resentment or defiance. When such attacks are made on him, it takes superhuman charity to remain unaffected and to carry one's messages without malice.

4.   Watchdog at the Gates

If there is a certain nobility in the connection between journalists and popes, there is a good deal of ambivalence in the link between journalists and dogs. We may like to think of ourselves as newshounds, but we don't really like the image of a pack of pariahs snarling over carrion in the gutter. And yet we say 'Dog doesn't eat dog', meaning one journalist doesn't criticise another – an odd remark, since it is neither flattering nor strictly true nor, again, particularly worthy. Why shouldn't a journalist, who criticises everybody else, be open to criticism by his fellows? However, there is another canine image which I think we all rather fancy: that of the watchdog.

I have said the mass media have the function of an early warning system to society, though to tell the truth the warnings more often come too late than too soon. Most journalists have their noses down to the events of the day; they have little time to look ahead and see what is coming. Moreover, events now move so fast and are so complex that accurate prediction is more a matter of luck than skill. Who would have forecast the growth of a coloured immigrant problem in Britain, the arrival of Cuban troops in Ethiopia, the fall of Beirut, the rise of Libya, the embracing of Mao Tse-tung by Richard M. Nixon? If God moves in a mysterious way his wonders to perform, he gives no advance notice to the media.

Yet if journalists have little success as prophets in the sense of forecasters, they have a good deal more in the sense of being analysts of the situation whose duty it is to declare how they see things. At this point I make further distinctions within the terms I am using. There is hardly such a thing as a journalist in general: he is normally an editor, a sub-editor (who rewrites and arranges the text that is sent in), a reporter or a correspondent – a correspondent being a senior reporter who specialises in a particular subject and is responsible for seeing that his organisation is kept informed about it. To these you might add rarer breeds of journalist like the leader writer (who composes the policy editorials, often after consultation with the paper's top men) and the columnist who occupies a vague territory somewhere between the correspondent and the leader writer. Broadcasting has its own oddities like the anchorman or presenter, who strings together the items in a magazine programme, and the interviewer who tries to persuade people in the news to do the journalist's job for him by telling all in their own voices.

Few of these will find themselves often in the role of prophets or watchdogs, for most journalism is routine, humdrum stuff, even though journalists struggle, sometimes too hard, to make it seem of vital importance. There is little doubt that we could survive with duller media, or at least duller newspapers, than we are accustomed to, if only editors would judge things by their longer significance rather than their immediate catchiness, and if readers could come to accept headlines that were soberly informative rather than jazzily entertaining.

The vast majority of what appears in the media is simply a public service, like the gas, the water and the electricity, which are there to be used if you want them and ignored if you don't. And such a service is provided in Britain with a fair degree of reliability and skill, from sports results to weather forecasts and stockmarket prices. In fact few countries are so well served with such plain, basic information. There is also a steady flow of factual news of a more varied kind, outbreaks of disease, transport delays, jobs opening and closing, prices rising and falling, legislation passed or pending, all of which is useful to some concerned section of the public.

Again, there is a good deal of pure entertainment in the media, and I would not make much distinction here between the obviously fictitious strip cartoons (which nobody pretends any more are just for the children) and real life reporting of the SIXTH FORM SEX LESSON WENT TOO FAR variety. One might, one just might, argue that stories like that are designed to warn parents of the advancing debauchery of our school system, but I doubt if anyone really believes it. This is the kind of sexy entertainment that sells newspapers and takes readers' minds off the dreadfulness of the more serious news, about which they can do nothing. Is frivolous, sexy news harmful or un-Christian? There is a good deal about modesty and lust in the Christian tradition, and I should be surprised to see such items in, say, the *Church Times* or the *Friend*. But the fact is the very appearance of those perky nudes on page three of the *Sun* tells us we aren't really living in a Christian context at all, but in a more or less pagan one.

You are entitled to argue with the paper that the nudes are degrading to womanhood (though I notice plenty of women checking their own figures by them), devalue sex or incite to lasciviousness, but not, I think, that they are violating a *religious* code of morality to which most of the paper's readers and writers don't subscribe. It is almost as futile as complaining about a front page photo of the Prime Minister on the grounds that Islam forbids the representation of the human form. One would expect an avowedly Christian photographer not to take titillating nudes, and an avowedly Christian reader not to buy them, but until the number of Christians on newspapers and among the public increases, we shall continue to have a pagan press – and enjoy it. For (let's not face it) most of us are more than half pagan and so enjoy the media.

I am doubtful, then, whether there is much point in journalism setting itself up as the watchdog of public morality, seeing that we have entered a world in which anything which is not illegal is, apparently, not immoral. And yet this is not quite so: there are still cases in which a jury has to decide, and where juries are brought in there is still room for public opinion to make itself felt. I have myself sat upon juries which have come to the conclusion, 'The accused probably did it, but the accusers are such bastards they deserved it' – and acquitted. So that a social code of ethics does still count. And here the mass media do have a role to play.

The trouble here is that a journalist who does not present himself as the spokesman for a political party or a church is hard put to it to be accepted as more than just a literate and possibly interesting individual. A few columnists – I think of Alistair Cooke, Bernard Levin and Eric Sevareid – have managed to establish themselves in that way, and they have done so through a mixture of style and intelligence. They work on essentially the same material as everyone else, but they draw more interesting conclusions from it and they do so more elegantly. It calls for experience as well as talent. Mr Cooke, for example, has seen every American president since Hoover in action. That he has been allowed to stay on the air so long is something of a mystery, since the current philosophy of man management in broadcasting is to get rid of the oldies and keep the young men on the move, lest they settle down and become boring old experts.

But what gives the journalist the right to set himself up as a watchdog? The question may be put by an impatient editor or an aggrieved politician, and it is hard to answer. 'The prerogative of the harlot – power without responsibility' is often quoted, with the addition: 'After all, whom does the journalist represent – who elected *him*?' This implies that the politician, who is usually complaining, *has* been elected to represent – well, whom? And to what extent? Does he represent the entire adult population of his constituency, or just those who voted for him? And does he represent them on the basic issues of the election, or on all the small print of the party manifesto – including, perhaps, a pledge to nationalise the hotel industry or to seat two red-bearded dwarves on the board of every Quango in the land? Because if he does – and the election is thus more of a plebiscite than a choice of representative – there is little point in making editorial comment on the conduct of government at all.

I wrote earlier that in the United States the media fill a real gap in the constitution and are vital to the efficient running of the Republic. Even though we do not care to admit it, there are similar gaps in the British constitution. Consider the role of the media in the Watergate Affair, and in the publication of the Pentagon Papers which revealed to the American public the long history of deception below the surface of the war in Vietnam. In Britain, the truth about the Suez adventure, the avoidance of Rhodesian oil sanctions, the corruption of the

Inner London police, the plight of the thalidomide babies in their struggle for compensation, would have been swept under the carpet but for media investigations. Britain's provincial newspapers have a long and honourable record of keeping watch over local government and of monitoring the tempting relationships between local councillors and local business. This kind of supervision ought indeed to be exercised by the elected representatives of the people themselves, rather than by the media. But at the national level, select committees are sadly ill-equipped to confront the Whitehall monster; while locally it may be hard for councillors to look critically upon the activities of their own intimate chums.

Exposure journalism does not make the media any more popular. There are still those who would excuse President Nixon's sinister abuse of his presidential powers and write off Lyndon Johnson's deception of the people as having been 'in the national interest', much as the supporters of Sir Anthony Eden did after Suez. What that implies is that the end does justify the means, so long as it is painted red, white and blue.

Patriotism of that kind is the refuge not of scoundrels but of men who dare not admit a mistake. To such men the journalist has to represent the Franciscan penitentiary who used to confront the Pope at his coronation, thrusting forward a hank of burning flax and crying 'Thus passes the glory of the world.' Politicians are less ready to hear intimations of their fallibility than popes. A friend of mine who was advising one of our national leaders on his public relations suggested that it might be effective if, once in a while, he was to admit having made some error. It would make him seem more human. 'I entirely agree,' said the great man with enthusiasm; and then added, after a pause, 'The trouble is, I can't think of any mistakes I have made.'

Now that party politics can be seen and heard as an exchange of supposed infallibilities that cannot possibly all be true – and are therefore to some degree false – the journalist is the nearest thing to an objective figure on the stage. The government masses behind itself the machinery of the civil service, and the opposition, though less well equipped, has some kind of research establishment to check the official version. But how objective can the opposition afford to be? In the nature of party politics, it is hardly likely to issue findings that confirm government policy. What is more, the opposition's whole reason for being, under the British system, is not to facilitate a fixed term in office for the government, but to offer a continuous alternative and to seek to overthrow that government at the earliest possible moment. The opposition, then, may be as negative and ungenerous as the government is arrogant and deaf to criticism. It is said this is the only way party morale and discipline can be maintained. The clash between absolutely yes and absolutely no is held to produce firm and authoritative government. From the passion of some politicians for firmness, you might think that Britain was an ill-developed and unruly country, instead of one of the more mature and better-behaved.

Given our system – and there are much worse in the world – you can hardly expect greater frankness. But, as we have seen recently in cases like the Rhodesian oil sanctions (which were never really applied or enforced even by Britain herself) the system does breed hypocrisy and self-deception, and its periodic exposure causes deepening cynicism on the part of the public. It is not that our politicians are evil men on the make. One of the concerns of the Christian journalist ought to be to show what appalling lives they are obliged to lead – underpaid, overworked, deprived of anything like reasonable family lives. It is not surprising if men of the highest abilities look away from such poorly rewarded and ill-regarded work. Politicians have themselves to blame for much of this; for encouraging the assumption, for example, that a public servant who never rests is to be preferred to one who works human hours. But it would help if the media did present them as human beings. And this has to include watching out for signs of self-deceptive special pleading and the sort of one-sidedness that this highly competitive way of life encourages.

The journalist should not, I think, assume that all power is evil and corrupting. Acton went too far when he concluded his celebrated aphorism with 'Great men are almost always bad

61

men.' He would have done better to say, 'But you cannot lead without a capacity for ruthlessness.'

In my experience, most politicians want power because it enables them to get things done. They genuinely believe that what they want to do will be of service to their fellow men. And often it is, or might be if they did not have to make crippling compromises with circumstances. With the best will in the world, it is hard for the modern politician to master circumstances in the time usually available to him. And if the politician promises too much it is largely because the rest of us demand too much – especially the commentators of the mass media. We encourage the public to believe that if only this policy had been pursued instead of that policy, all would have been well and we should not have been in our present mess. The likelihood is, we should have been in a different one.

Watchdogging is something to be done more in sorrow than in anger, for it frequently means hurting somebody – the scientist who thought he had produced a beneficial drug but failed to test it adequately for side-effects, the local politician who slipped without noticing it from helping his old friends to accepting bribes, the civil servant whose attempts to cover up a single mistake have snowballed into a complex fraud. It is possible for the journalist to become thick-skinned about such exposures, but he can only do so by converting the victim, in his imagination, into something less than human, a caricature, a social or political symbol.

This is the great danger that lies behind politically inspired watchdogging, especially of the extreme left or right. The victim becomes a Trotskyite traitor or a capitalist tycoon, and immediately he is branded as incapable of any normal human feelings. Worse still, it is implied that unless he is identified with the writer's party, the victim is quite incapable of redemption. The whole concept of objectivity, of liberal pluralism is attacked at its very roots, and it is particularly disturbing to find this attitude taking hold in classes of communication studies and theoretical journalism. (I have to admit that, as one who has never actually *studied* the way he makes his living, I am extremely doubtful of the theoretical approach.)

62

That dog increasingly does eat dog is borne out by some of the journals of our trade, in which excellence as a journalist often seems to be of less interest than the correct political stance, and where militancy counts for more than literacy. Few professional journals seem more remote from the product of the profession than the journals of journalism. They appear to be written largely by people who have given up the craft or achieved little prominence in it: the public would recognise few names that claim to speak there for the media.

One of the persistent complaints to be read in journalistic journals is that the media of Britain are controlled by aristocratic proprietors who are 'anti-worker, anti-democratic and anti-labour'. Papers, it is said, pretend to represent their readers while in fact under capitalist law, a newspaper owner can do what he likes with his editorial control. Do we really believe that Lord Thomson, Lord Hartwell, Lord Rothermere, Lord Cowdray and Lord Gibson are interested in forwarding the interests of the British trade unionist and the Labour Party? Their one obsession, say the critics on the left, is knocking the trade unions and the government, which amounts to knocking Britain.

I have not the least wish to favour any side politically in this book. If I am right in believing that a Christian journalist should always lean away from the snap popular judgment, searching in charity for the redeeming features of the unpopular, and ready to revise his own views, then it follows that he will make an unreliable party politician. I could have written a passage carefully balancing the one above, in which I would have displayed the conviction of some right-of-centre commentators that the media, and broadcasting in particular, have been infiltrated by leftists whose knocking of Britain takes the form of sneering at the Conservative party and business leadership. It seems to me that what both sides are really complaining about is that the mass media are disturbingly volatile in their likes and dislikes, unreliable in their political impact.

If the predominantly Conservative ownership of Fleet Street (and management of broadcasting) were truly influential, there should not have been a single Labour government this century.

For there has never been a time when Tory-owned papers had anything but a huge majority of the total circulation. Yet, especially since 1945, Labour has won at least its fair share of elections, regardless of front page bias. And there is little doubt in my mind that, even making allowances for sincere conviction, there *has* been deliberate bias against the left in most papers. Others, while making it clear where they stand in their leader pages, have made remarkably balanced presentations in their news columns. The unpleasant suspicion that I have is that nothing would satisfy the far left except a blatant bias leftwards in all departments.

Would that even be profitable? I doubt it. It seems to me an illusion that elections are decided by the newspapers – or even the television. For a start, few people who buy a newspaper bother to read the editorial columns; and most people buy a particular paper not so much because it represents their views as because it provides them with what they need without actively annoying them. If there is one thing that annoys the sceptical British reader, it is the kind of evangelical politics that the extreme left would like to see in a newspaper of its own. There is a great deal wrong with Fleet Street's Tory press, but unswerving loyalty to Tory leaders and doctrines is not part of it. Since the death of the late Lord Beaverbrook, none of my Fleet Street friends has told me of any orders to distort the news; and Tory papers seem to have been as willing to expose fraud in the boardroom as they have been to report bloody-mindedness on the shopfloor.

Why the left, or the Trades Union Congress, does not raise the funds to launch a daily paper of its own is hard to understand – if they really believe that papers are so influential. Harder still to understand, because it would cost so much less, is their failure to make friends of the existing media. Some sections, in fact, have done so. For example, one sees little adverse criticism of postmen largely because their union leadership goes out of its way to welcome and confide in reporters, who are then prepared to listen sympathetically to the postmen's case.

Journalists would not have to appoint themselves as watchdogs, would not have to pose as prophets of doom, if those who govern us and supply our goods and services would open themselves to the public – inevitably through the media – and would treat journalists as potential friends rather than *prima facie* enemies. I shall have more to say about this when I come to deal with the journalist's relations with government; but what I must say now is that until authority at all levels can bring itself to operate openly, it will invite both malpractice in its own ranks and suspicion in the mass media. When authority operates in secret, it is easy to hide corruption. When it is known to be open, it will be far less harassed by people wondering what it is up to.

There could be few better examples of this than Washington's Watergate Affair, a case of two young journalists relentlessly following back an apparently trivial burglary until it was revealed as the logical development of the President's obsession with power at any price. Today, already, some voices are to be heard saying that Nixon was misunderstood, that he was simply playing tough in an excess of patriotism; but it seems to me that he stands exposed for ever as a man whose excessive doubts and fears, whose determination to win at all costs and belief that he was above the law unfitted him for high office. Not only did he lie to his people, he was prepared to use the secret intelligence and security services as tools of his personal political ambition. And none of this would have come to light if two reporters on the *Washington Post* had not appointed themselves watchdogs of the public interest.

It is a sobering and at times lonely position to hold. For while I write of the need for authority to make friends with journalists, the fact is that a journalist dares not return that friendship too cordially. The time may come when he has to print or broadcast something that will pain the man who has befriended him, and judging that moment may well drive a Christian journalist to his knees. There have been occasions in my own career when people who have been very good to me as sources of information have come to me and said, 'I understand you know *this* – I appeal to you not to broadcast it, for the following reason.' Obviously a lot has depended on the reason. In one case it was argued that men's lives were in danger. Since there was no

65

posibility that broadcasting what I knew would have saved any *other* lives, I did not hesitate: I withdrew my broadcast. What was more, I genuinely liked and respected the man who had appealed to me and it seemed to me of greater moral value to do him a favour than to supply millions of listeners with what, to most of them, would have been no more than a titbit of useless information. But there have been other occasions when I felt I was being asked to cover up incompetence affecting the safety of the public, or, in one case, cruelty to prisoners; and so I rejected the appeals and sacrificed the friendships.

For confronting the enquiring reporter, all the time, are the questions, 'Does this really matter?' and 'If I don't – who will?' It is easy enough to dismiss the dilemma by arguing that it is not for the reporter to worry about repercussions and that it is up to his editor to decide whether or not to publish. I have already drawn a comparison with the pursuit of scientific truth 'for its own sake'. But news does not exist for its own sake: it becomes news both because it is 'that which is new' and because it matters to someone. The reporter cannot, I think, avoid asking himself whether it is of greater importance that it be published or be ignored. Who will benefit? Who will be harmed? And where does the moral balance lie? For I do not believe the Christian journalist should write off the moral aspects of his job. Mere entertainment, excitement or amusement are not good enough reasons for making people miserable, for hounding and pestering them – though other demands may be, where those concerned are strong and responsible enough to stand up to the enquiries. Nor should those enquiries be rude or dishonest: I think they seldom are, and such behaviour is firmly forbidden by every journalists' code of ethics I have ever read. But perhaps Christian journalists should ask themselves more often whether they can conscientiously accept certain assignments. If anyone were threatened with dismissal as a result, there should be an interesting test case before the appeals tribunal.

In the end the journalist cannot really shift the responsibility for the moral content of his work on to his editor, any more than a Nazi war criminal could plead 'superior orders'. The question

'If I don't – who will?' can have two meanings. It can mean 'If I expose, or fail to expose, this news – will it ever come to light at all?' or it can mean 'If I do not handle this with all the understanding I can muster, will it be passed on to a journalist with less restraint?' It *can* be a journalist's moral duty to report something that he knows and which turns his stomach; or to report as best he can something which he believes would better rest unknown – except that it is bound to be known sooner or later. As a practical rule, one learns that it is seldom much good to try and keep news; like fish, it goes off rapidly once it has been caught. It is also bad policy to fancy oneself as the defender and champion of some great public cause. A watchdog barks when he senses the household threatened, but it is not necessarily for him to advise the householders precisely how to react to the threat. In short, ideologically motivated reporters are a pain in the neck.

5. Public Relations for Terror

In Belfast, a Provo bomber leaves a shopping bag in a restaurant and tiptoes away, leaving a random score of housewives to be blown apart. At Lydda airport, in Israel, Japanese machine-gunners, hired by Palestine Arabs, mow down a flock of Puerto Rican Catholic pilgrims. In Rhodesia, African nationalist guerrillas round up the shocked survivors of a crashed airliner and slaughter them. And in rural England, a gang of burglars, caught in the act by a newspaper boy, shoot him in the head.

Violence is in fashion, or everyone believes that it is. It scarcely matters to us today that England was far more violent in the eighteenth century and the late middle ages (as research into manorial and court registers has demonstrated). People are convinced that if only we could identify the cause of the violence around them – or *said* to be around them, for very few actually experience it – then we could eliminate it and return to a normal state of peace and reason. At present the favourite villains are the mass media – the press, radio, cinema and above all television. They are accused of glorifying criminals, of popularising violence, of providing the public relations for terror. If only they could be restrained, it is implied, violence would vanish.

To my mind the saddest of heresies is that there can be any simple explanation for complex events. Human motives are almost always mixed and there is no simple causative chain starting at A and running direct to B. The problem of violence is a very ancient and particularly complex one, far older than print and broadcasting. Throughout history its tide has ebbed and flowed, flooding now this country and now that. Mostly people have taken it for granted. Our horror of it is a comparatively recent development, and some of our ancestors would probably have thought us soft and naîve.

As I declared in the introduction to this book, I am a Quaker, a member of the Religious Society of Friends, which means that I passionately detest violence and try to do what I can for the cause of non-violence and peace. I took this decision largely as a result of my experiences as a reporter, in particular during the US ghetto riots of the 1960s and in the Vietnam War. But I do not believe that the media I served helped to create that violence, unless it can be said that a failure of communications – of which they were a part – led to the frustration that exploded in those riots and that war.

Because I feel this problem is central to the functions of journalism, I am going to make a digression from journalism as such and take a look at certain aspects of man as communicator.

There are those who maintain that man is inherently a violent animal, that he is the only creature that will viciously attack his own kind. But this is not altogether true: if you keep many animals in confusing, unnatural and overcrowded conditions, they too will destroy their young, savage their relatives and engage in sexual perversions. One of the important distinctions between human violence and the violence of the beasts is that, in natural surroundings, most animals have learnt to ritualise their conflicts – to turn them into relatively harmless engagements whose outcome is a foregone conclusion, but where face is saved all round.

Most animal conflicts arise out of what has been termed the territorial imperative: the urge of the male animal to mark out and defend a territory which is generally speaking just big enough to provide him and his mate and family with food and security. He is literally *programmed* to drive out any intruder, and the intruder, knowing he is in the wrong, usually puts up only a token resistance before retreating.

Now man is certainly part animal, and he gets into deep trouble when he tries to deny this. We all have our programmed instincts and defending our home and family is one of them. Man is, of course, much more than a zoo beast. He does have certain powers of choice. He has the ability to look at himself, approve or criticise himself and devise an image of himself he wants to live up to. That image is conditioned by all kinds of

69

social and parental influences. But each of us has someone he wants to be. And he wants others to accept and recognise that image, to accord it as much respect as its owner does. That is what it means to find one's place in life, to identify one's place in the pecking order; for notwithstanding liberty, equality and fraternity, we all belong to some system of inequalities.

I do not believe that man really is a violent creature by nature – for one thing, his soft body and lack of natural weapons leave him extremely badly equipped for violence. What I do believe is that man is an extremely talented and ambitious creature, too clever for his own good. His intelligence has run miles ahead of his emotions, and he has built himself a world in which he is a stranger. For example, whereas a century ago a reporter might have been able – with the help of a horse – to conduct one leisurely interview in a day, he can now – with the aid of a car, aircraft and satellite – provide in the same day a report on the Lambeth Conference in Canterbury for the *World at One*, followed by an eyewitness account of the laying-in-state of a Pope in Rome for the nine o'clock news. We talk about labour-saving devices, but I think they result in our taking on more problems, decisions, choices and judgments, and having to make more adjustments to new situations than we are really designed to take. Add to this the strain of crowded city life, of constantly having to interact with total strangers, to worry about whether our children are getting killed by one of those labour-saving devices – a life we live without the support of an extended family or close community – and what surprises me is not that people blow up from time to time, but that they can control themselves at all.

And what does all this mean in terms of my theories of violence and communication? I repeat that man is ambitious to make his mark and be accepted as significant *in some field*. We don't all have to be Prime Minister or even shop steward; just to be the best goalkeeper in the village, or the man who can always be relied on to make people laugh, or the street's expert at fixing motorbikes – that will do. Our lives are spent telling people what we think we are, and watching eagerly to see if they have got the signal. Most of our actions are attempts to *say* something, more than *do* something. Even a man who chops down a tree is saying, 'I am the strong man who can master a tree with his skill.'

Just so, violence is a language. It is the language people use when all other languages – words and deeds – have failed. What the violence says is not necessarily right. It may be wicked or evil or nonsense – or justified. The point is that before violence is resorted to, there has been a breakdown in normal communications. And this is where the media of mass communication are so important. For they should stand between us and violence.

There are various ways in which a breakdown in communications can take place. It may be, as violent protests often claim, that the 'other side' (authority) has refused to listen to verbal representations, or has listened and rejected them as not worth taking seriously. It may be that the protestor cannot express himself adequately. Or – and this is one of the curses of the age – it may be that even though they both appear to be speaking English, the two sides simply don't think in the same terms or accept each other's concepts.

For language can be undermined, perverted, distorted, biased, even neglected. You can take a word like *profit*, *capitalist*, *élite*, *people's democracy*, *police*, *race*, *left-wing* or even *peace* and poison it, so that no one dares use it any more in its proper sense. To anyone who uses words in the old way, the new way becomes a foreign language and the person who speaks it becomes a foreigner, incapable of understanding or being understood any more.

One of the essentials for violence is that each side must regard the other as alien, different from itself. The police, for example, will become fair game for killers if they can be turned into stuffed uniforms with numbers on their shoulders, robots controlled by a ruling class. For if the terrorist could see his victim as a fellow human being with feelings and a family, like himself, he would have to be a psychopath in the strictest medical sense of the word to be able to pull the trigger. But the use of revolutionary jargon which the other side does not share helps to maintain the necessary alienation, makes violence sustainable, and the leaders of violent revolution know this. They *must*

71

keep their followers from speaking the same language as the rest of us, or fraternisation might set in and understanding replace hatred.

What I am pleading for is fluency in a common language. I find it alarming that, even in our universities there are so many young people who have difficulty in expressing themselves, and that behind them are often more articulate people who denounce reasoned discussion as 'a bourgeois illusion'. To quote the theologian Anthony Hanson, 'There is a divide between rationalists and irrationalists. In the rationalist camp are Christians and many humanists, liberal Marxists and anti-materialist scientists. In the other camp are to be found followers of Freud and orthodox Marxists who are surely destined for the sort of power nihilism of Nietzsche. We must choose between these two, and we ought to choose the side of reason.'

Whether the corruption of language comes through ignorance or design, communication is choked off by it. What follows is frustration, and it is the frustration, the failure to get one's message through, that leads directly to violence. Some outbursts of fury are easy enough to understand. But not all frustration is the result of a direct command 'Thou shalt not'. It may build up over a period of time. It may take the form of a lack of opportunity. It may be the absence of stimulation or challenge, so that the personality has nothing to bring it to life. It may result from the lack of opposition. It may be sheer boredom that is frustrating. All of these can thwart one's ambition to make one's mark. And as a result the language of violence may be saying a variety of these things: 'Help, I can't cope!' 'I'm the boss in these parts!' 'Let me out of this lousy place!' 'Go away, stranger!' 'I despise women!' 'To hell with respectability!' Or even, 'Love me!'

If what I say is so – and I firmly believe that it is – then a variety of things follow, which I will sum up in advance by saying that while the mass media *could* contribute to terrorism and violence, in fact they do not; and that they have an almost sacred responsibility to remain in that path. In particular they are charged with preserving the sanctity of language.

Let me relate what I believe about language and violence to the functions of the media. If it is true that violence can only flourish where people have been alienated from each other and taught to regard other races and creeds as less than human, then the media clearly are not guilty in two situations with which most of my readers will be familiar – Northern Ireland and the English black ghettos. It simply is not possible to name any newspaper, any broadcasting network, which has persistently tried to denigrate one group or incite another. They have either kept all too silent about the situation or laboured positively for understanding, sometimes to the distaste of their readers and listeners. There has been nothing printed or broadcast in Britain that remotely approaches the output of Nazi Germany or Fascist Italy. Whoever is to blame for the burning of Catholic housing by Protestant mobs or the bashing of Bengalis by white gangs in the East End of London, it cannot be the media.

Again, if it is true that man's real object in life is to be recognised as a significant member of his community, and that frustration and violence set in when he fails to secure that, then the media must be one of the principle positive forces. For they are the vehicles of recognition, the platforms on which people stand recognised. Quite simply, people like to get their names in the papers, as any reporter knows who has written a sports report or taken down the lists at weddings and funerals.

Further, if violence is the language of last resort, the media often do gallant service as the last but one. President Sadat's extraordinary offer to go to Jerusalem to meet Prime Minister Begin of Israel was prompted by a newspaper interviewer. The Marshall Plan that restored Western Europe economically after World War II might never have been launched if a small group of British correspondents had not drawn attention to General Marshall's first tentative kite-flying. And time and again, during periods of diplomatic non-communication, Washington, Moscow and Peking have signalled to one another by way of editorials, press releases and published speeches. A French ambassador once confided to me that if he had to choose between his diplomatic cables and his daily papers as sources of information, he would always choose the newspapers.

Today the intimate, human reporting of one country to another by resident correspondents is the best defence against the heresy that wogs begin at Calais – or, for that matter, at Bradford. Every report that dehumanises its subject, turns human beings into caricatures who are not to be taken seriously, is in effect setting them up for hatred, ridicule, contempt and in extreme cases murder. It is not easy to persuade Mrs Brinkley of Brixton to *love* Idi Amin of Uganda, but at least she can be helped to appreciate his point of view and not dismiss it as inevitably less sensible than her own. What is probably more important is that Mrs Brinkley should take seriously the point of view of Mumtaz Bibi, her next-door neighbour in Brixton, who wears such peculiar clothes, cooks such pungent food and doesn't even try to speak English. Perhaps the media have done too little to build this particular bridge, but I think it is true to say that the media have done at least as much as the churches in active support of racial understanding in Britain. They have done more than most institutions, I think, to prevent alienation.

But what about the charge that the media 'glorify' criminals, and bathe terrorists in the floodlight of publicity?

It comes down to the theory that the wicked would not flourish if they received no publicity at all. But do we really believe that the IRA would shrivel up if they were not in the nine o'clock news? I have tried hard to understand those who do believe this. I think their feelings begin with a natural reaction. We hear of the IRA Provisionals threatening to murder judges but we would not admit, as Britishers, to being personally fearful at this. I don't believe either that it intimidates the judges, any more than Nazi threats during World War II made the British surrender; but it does make us angry and resentful. We don't like hearing that sort of talk – it ought to be stopped – and by a rather sloppy elision of thought that becomes 'It ought not to be published.' You might argue that the IRA ought not to be given the satisfaction of seeing it published. But that seems to me a fairly trivial satisfaction in exchange for what is really of importance to the rest of the community: that we be put on our guard against what the terrorists intend, and that we get some evidence towards making our personal judgment on what kind of people they are. If we publish their claims and threats – commenting on them from the other side, if need be – then they stand exposed not necessarily as high-minded patriots or devout Roman Catholics but (it may be) as sick-minded, low-grade conspirators who have trapped themselves in a dead end. But this, surely, has to emerge from the facts as best the media can find and present them. It cannot emerge by passing a law saying, 'From now on, all IRA men will be referred to as sick-minded low-grade conspirators.'

Part of the prejudice against 'giving publicity' to terrorists is that the word 'publicity' suggests in itself the selling of something desirable. But that is not what the media are doing at all; what they are doing is providing communications. I once shocked a class of policemen by telling them that terrorists ought to have communications like everybody else; first because if they are talking they are a little less likely to bomb and kill; second because we need some idea of what they are up to; and third because not all terrorists are wrong all the time, and what they *say* is a great deal less likely to be wrong than what they *do*.

Even a pacifist – no, a pacifist *in particular* – should recognise that terrorism must be rooted in some sort of grievance. Anyone who doubts that England has, over the centuries, treated Ireland with every vicious quality from brutality to neglect is, perhaps, fortunate in his innocence. Governments, universities and media together might even avert future violence if they would apply such lessons to the present and learn to identify the ripening symptoms of revolt. History suggests that the most violence-prone states are those at the extremes, those which are extremely authoritarian and those which are extremely permissive: moderate democracies seem to be the least susceptible to terrorism. Further, violence tends to strike not when human suffering is at its worst, but when conditions have been improving for some time and then encounter an unexpected setback.

The media observer has to be careful to distinguish between widespread popular revolt, which is very rare, and minority terrorism against foreign rule or against domestic oppression. It

75

is the dream of the terrorist faction to kindle and lead the great people's revolt; but the faction is usually far less representative of the people than it likes to pretend. It is especially important for tender-hearted liberals to be able to recognise when a so-called liberation army is really spear-heading the suppressed aspirations of the downtrodden, and when it is creature of its own ideological fantasies. A strain of hysterical paranoia in the leadership can speedily convince a movement that a society which is no worse than casually unfair is deliberately oppressive. It is not a question which would go down well at a protest rally, but the question should be put to every would-be revolutionary. Are things really so bad that only revolution can bring improvement – or are we all just bored? And beyond that we should ask if revolution ever *does* bring real improvement; whether the price is worth paying. The precedents are not encouraging.

Revolutionaries desperately need their myths and their martyrs, and it is amazing, and depressing, how often authority obliges by supplying them. After the black ghetto riots in America in the 1960s, commissions of enquiry found time after time that the forces of the law and order had made matters worse than they need have been by charging in, armed, intimidating and displaying a total absence of everyday humour and humanity. In effect, they obligingly completed the alienation. And that is the real meaning of the so-called politics of confrontation – to force the other side into brutality, if it won't go voluntarily. Tolerant government must be made intolerant, and one which persists in treating terrorists as ordinary criminals subject to ordinary law must be panicked into passing special regulations, reviving cruel and unusual punishments and suspending normal civil rights. Then it can be accused of oppression. Against all this, the reporter must beware and must warn all who will listen to him.

To bind itself together, give itself shape and identity, and convince itself that it is working for more than selfish ends, the revolutionary band must have a political philosophy. Life is, in fact, enormously complex and difficult to explain. Yet we seize gratefully at simple explanations, not because they are accurate but because here at last is something we can grasp. The simplicity of witchcraft, racism, anti-semitism, anti-imperialism, college communism has been their greatest appeal. And simplicity is an important factor among young, medium-educated people today: many of them cannot stand the altitude of the academic heights to which they are pushed, they get fed up with the endless talk and they look for something easier. They look for action.

To many revolutionaries and terrorists the chief appeal of violence is its directness and simplicity: they see it as pure and uncompromising, expressing the commitment and responsibility of the individual. Violence is not just a means of liberation, it is a liberating experience in itself, for it asserts that the purpose of man is not to argue but to act. Thus to the revolutionary, war is beautiful, it is really living. What is bad is weakness, the refusal to take violent action. Furthermore, violence becomes almost a religious experience, a baptism. And the terrorist knows the secret weakness of the law-abiding middle-class citizen: that he is afraid of pain and highly susceptible to systematic violence.

The terrorist uses violence to bring us all down to the level on which he alone is a specialist. Once violence is applied against us, the temptation is to lose our temper, cast aside reason and hit back. Increasingly, in violent situations, people want only to listen to their own arguments, and they will argue that since reason has apparently failed, counter-violence is the only answer. This offers a hell-sent opportunity for the aggressive, anti-social young people whom society has rejected. The natural killer, who may be good for very little else, at last gains his recognition, and people are caught up in the spiral of violence without understanding its causes. The whole history of Ulster for the past 70 years and more bears witness to this, as it does, to the self-perpetuating non-solution of violence.

All of this, it seems to me, it is the duty of the media to observe and report: to expose the frustrations and disappointments, the myths (whether true or false); it is their duty to stop governments and people from losing their heads and supplying terrorists with justification, whether it is by beating up prisoners or discriminating against coloured people. It is the duty of the media, too, to discover and analyse what the revolutionaries are adopting as their philosophy, to point out the true complexity of things, to expose the over-simplifications and falsehoods, to resist the heresy that all argument, and even language itself, must serve 'the cause', rather than any objective standard of reason and meaning.

For there *are* such standards, and we have to resist the heresy that argument and language are the slaves of class or economic interests. Thus I believe it is dangerous to allow the term 'violence' to be applied to something which is really callous or thoughtless or incompetent. I have heard it said, for example, that 'low wages are violence against the poor' or that 'bad housing amounts to violence against the working class'. Violence is physical force used (some would add 'illegitimately') by one human being against another; and it has such horrific implications that it seems to me gravely irresponsible to apply the word so loosely. It is one of those words bursting with overtones like *massacre, horror, bloodbath, rape, mugging, disaster, crisis, inferno, torture*, even *terrorist* itself, and a host of others. They need to be handled by journalists today with the greatest of care.

Do we then, in the media, oblige the terrorist (patriot? freedom-fighter?) with the publicity he wants? If he blows up a restaurant and telephones the radio to announce that he has done it to demoralise the idle rich and discredit the police, does the radio serve the interests of terrorism by broadcasting that claim? Or should there be some form of censorship?

In fact the media exercise much more restraint and hold back more at the request of the authorities than the public seems to realise. During recent kidnappings, bombings and the celebrated Balcombe Street siege of an IRA gang, the media were in continuous voluntary co-operation with the police – and were thanked for it. By no means every terrorist claim goes on the air, just as most of the horrific pictures that arrive at television news studios end up on the cutting-room floor. Journalists do have some taste and judgment, as well as a running knowledge of what their public (or its more articulate members) will stand

78

for. They also have lawyers and MPs breathing down their necks.

The real case against a formalised censorship of the news is that nobody can possibly be trusted to eliminate items objectively, rather than to make them fit a politically conceived pattern. And once you begin cutting the news to a pattern, you might as well hand over the media to the governing party. The fact that we do not do so in Britain has a lot to do with general equanimity in times of trial. By and large people trust the media, and even the authorities are coming to learn that the media are not just a nuisance under their feet, but media of communication and can themselves be communicated with like reasonable people.

Perhaps I should reinforce this chapter by a special defence of *television* against the charge of encouraging violence. I must confess that my heart is not entirely in this, not because I consider television to be guilty as charged but for various other reasons. I am concerned in this book with journalism, and most of the violence that appears on television occurs during films, plays, fiction series, which are not my department. Moreover, even as journalism I find television an unsatisfactory medium: bad at conveying ideas, demanding even more simplification of the complex than radio does, and altogether too clumsy and too expensive to work with compared with radio or print. I am not at all sure that the amount of money one has to spend to put the simplest piece of news on the screen doesn't involve one in some kind of sin.

However, I will say this about violence on television: a vast amount of research has been done on the connection between viewing violent television and committing acts of violence. A recent work by Professor Eysenck and Mr D. K. B. Nias asserts, 'Different methods of investigation all point to an association between viewing violence and subsequent aggression' and again that 'the evidence is fairly unanimous (*sic*) that aggressive acts new to the subject's repertoire of responses can be evoked by the viewing of violent scenes on television'. My own understanding is that while there may, indeed, be an *association* the evidence is very far from unanimous as to which

79

event comes first. Indeed in view of the enormous complexity of human life and motives it is almost impossible to think of any test that *could* be devised to prove that television is responsible for violence, rather than reflecting the violence that numerous other factors have bred in the life around us.

The report of the Surgeon General of the United States – still the most comprehensive on the subject – did find a small positive correlation between the two, but too small to be of any value. Some of the subsidiary research concluded that – Yes, violent people did like watching violent TV shows; but it did not follow the shows were responsible for their violence. In fact further research suggested that the real difference between violent viewers of violent TV and non-violent viewers was *the way they were brought up.* Kids whose fathers knocked them about and encouraged them to be tough and manly had a worse record of violence than those whose fathers encouraged gentleness and tolerance.

I can detect a dissatisfied shuffling among my readers at this sort of conclusion. People want to believe that television is responsible for violence and will even tell you 'It's commonsense', a faculty often indistinguishable from prejudice. They argue that if watching beautiful ladies using it sells soap, then watching handsome men doing it must spread violence. But it seems to me this doesn't follow. No one is *selling* violence, and selling the soap involves a great deal more than showing ladies using it. It involves, notably, stocking the shops with it so that when the customer walks in he recognises it as something desirable. People do not rush into the streets demanding *Palmolive*, any more than they hurry from the sitting-room to beat up the first old lady they meet.

Let me confine myself to violence on TV news. I will grant, because I have seen it done and done it myself, that a piece of news film with some violence in it will take precedence over a piece that has none. 'Punchup on Campus' made the nine o'clock news. 'Campus Returns to Normal' did not. And this is because television journalism has inevitably been attracted to the styles and standards of the surrounding programmes which are essentially entertainment – at the expense, I say, of sound journalistic standards. One is competing to attract the attention, first and foremost of a jaded editor, then of a viewer who is being fished for by experts.

Personally, I am torn two ways by violence on the news. First, I find violence so dreadful that I would sooner watch obscenity: it is a question of bad taste at a very high level. But second, I am so horrified by it that I am inclined to let people know it in the fullest detail, so that they will appreciate it in all its dreadfulness. Yet is one entitled to shock, to nauseate people? Maybe that's how life is – a small part of it; but have I the right to rub people's noses in it, to make my point?

And if I do – will it work? There were American reporters during the Vietnam War who tried to show the folks back home how terrible the war was, and who only succeeded in hardening their public to the spectacle. 'Tune in for tomorrow night's slaughter' seemed to be the message. It was not until the casualties included the boy next door that Americans began to consider the war as a moral issue. Not long ago a letter to the *Tablet* complained of the journalisation of Christianity and demanded to know whether it was right to reduce a centuries-old structure of theology and prayer and contemplation to a continuous flood of talkativeness, a day-to-day ephemeral ding-dong. This prompts me to the whole problem of the journalisation of many other subjects, terrorism and war among them. What journalists would say they were doing is keeping up a supply of information so that people can extract their own philosophies from it. They would certainly deny that they were cultivating violence and terror; on the contrary, they would hope that what they reported turned people against both by showing what they are really like. Yet I doubt if it is possible to do that. Even when I have helped to make such film myself, it has never lived up to the reality: how can it, when you cannot include the smell, the heat, the emotional shock and the total envelopment of the experience? And so what you show in the end diminishes the horror, makes it seem tame, not so bad after all.

This to me is the great moral dilemma of reporting terror and violence: to make it acceptable in the living-room is to falsify it; to make it half-way near the reality is to make it unendurable.

6. Heat and Light

Perhaps a Quaker journalist should be expected to search his conscience more often than most of his colleagues. The Society of Friends has a tradition of quietness and lack of ostentation. Its *Advices* – for Friends would never stand for commandments – include such pointed remarks as 'Seek to know an inward retirement ... Pray that you may be restrained from unnecessary and superficial words ... Avoid hurtful criticism ... Be discriminating in the use of radio and television and other means of information, persuasion and entertainment.' All of which might be taken as indicating that journalism is not an occupation for Quakers at all.

On the other hand, in addition to the peacemaking role which I have already traced, I can see many opportunities in journalism which the *Advices* appear to welcome and encourage. 'Live adventurously,' they urge, 'When you have a choice of employment, choose that which gives the fullest opportunity for the use of your talents in the service of God and your fellow men ... In your relations with others, exercise imagination, understanding and sympathy. Listen patiently, and seek whatever truth other people's opinions may contain for you. Think it possible you may be mistaken. In discussion, avoid hurtful and provocative language; do not allow the strength of your convictions to betray you into making statements or allegations that are unfair or untrue.' So, as I see it, a Quaker journalist is by no means a contradiction in terms – but a dishonest, unscrupulous or inflammatory Quaker journalist certainly should be.

I continue to worry, therefore, about the role of the media in public controversy. Are they provocative? Do they make statements and allegations that are unfair or untrue? Do they think it possible they may – just occasionally – be mistaken and (as the

Advices go on to advise) 'In industrial strife, racial enmity and international tension, stand firmly by Christian principles, seeking to foster understanding between individuals, groups and nations?'

The whole question of whether the media of mass communication generate more heat than light still lies at the root of this book, not easily resolved in spite of the chapters that have gone before. One local journalist who has often discussed the matter with me thinks my entire approach is hopelessly idealistic. 'What you ignore all the time,' he insists, 'is that most people – let alone most journalists – aren't Christian, or not in the high-minded way you want them to be, and that journalism is a business, a way of earning a living by selling something – not a cross between poetry and religion.'

I have to admit he has two excellent points there, though in the end I think they come down to the second: that for most newsmen and news organisations, the economics of life have to come first and bills have to be paid. I am a rare and fortunate case in being able to make a tolerable living out of telling other people what they ought to be doing – advice which, if they followed it, would probably make them bankrupt. For example, if I had my way, any new newspaper that was launched in Britain would contain large, beautifully composed photographs and long, beautifully written articles of rather old news. Some of my friends would buy it, but not the millions who would go on voting with their pennies for the *Sun*, the *Mirror* and the *Star*. The so-called 'quality' press in Britain has a circulation that is not to be sniffed at, but the facts seem to be that most people look to broadcasting for their basic news service and read a newspaper by way of diversion. It has even been put to me that the BBC has been unwittingly responsible for undermining Fleet Street by providing a service of news with which print cannot compete and to which it must therefore provide an alternative.

Even the quality press has been affected. As broadcasting takes over the basic functions of the daily paper, the daily gets forced back on to those of the Sunday paper, providing the special background articles. The Sunday papers are then obliged to take over the role of the weekly magazine, with its reviews and photo-features – leaving the magazines with very little left to do at all. Not that any level of the press is safe from the competition of broadcasting, for the broadcasters too can offer background articles and picture coverage and are constantly narrowing the gap between the original news event and their own news in depth.

It is possible to argue that newspapers simply should not worry about this: that they should do the best they can and rely on people's need to *see* the news in front of them and to read and re-read it at their own convenience and at their own speed. But we have to return to the economic facts of life – that a newspaper is not just a service, it is somebody's living and it is not going to be a very good living unless it is sold in large numbers. As I have said already, advertising revenue depends largely on numbers. Securing those numbers means competing for readers' attention and not just hoping for the loyal support of people who share the same view of the world as the editor.

And so the eye-catching game begins. At one end of the spectrum the *Guardian* plays it with its celebrated punning headlines; at the other, so do the London evening papers with their classic TV STAR IN SEX PROBE SHOCK posters. Most of us succumb to one appeal or the other, but either way what we are seeking is not news so much as entertainment. We do not really need to know what the minor quizmaster has been up to behind his wife's back. We are in no sense the wiser or richer for it, though I suppose we may feel morally superior when we have finished reading or at least glad not to have been caught the same way.

One result of the definition of news 'that which has changed – that which is eye-catching' is that people and events in the news tend to be the very opposite of those familiar to the audience, which means that (unless we are talking about the most routine of small town weeklies) news is not representative of everyday life. Criticisms of the media for failing to present life 'as it really is' are thus beside the point. Nobody seriously wants to read that their neighbour's car did not start this morning, let alone that it did. The trouble is, as my local journalist friend keeps telling me, a lot of small town news isn't really much more exciting. How is he to make people take an interest in it and buy his paper rather than the rival rag? Either by making events sound slightly more unusual than they really are ('Ten year-old car starts first time – Never fails, says owner'), or by the standard journalistic technique of building the story up a bit ('A snap survey of Penzance car-owners suggests that red cars start twice as easily as black ones – and white cars more easily still. Garage experts are baffled . . .').

Broadcasting is really no better. There can't be many radio correspondents who have not, in the recent past, been rung up by a duty editor desperate for something, anything, to fill the bulletin, and who has not prided himself on his professionalism in making some sow's ear sound quite silky. There are considerable dangers in that pride of professionalism. But even more dangerous than making something out of nothing can be making too much out of something that is already bad enough. I suspect that most broadcasters have something of the ham actor about them (I admit the charge myself) and a certain taste for the dramatic is part of their makeup. In our defence, we are trying at the same time to seize the attention of our editor and make sure our audience gets the point of our story. Because of the very nature of the medium - open to so many distractions and offering no opportunity to go back on what has already been said – broadcasters tend to pare their statements down to the barest, crudest minimum, with as few qualifications as possible. Though life, as I keep saying, isn't really like that at all.

Let me take an example of public controversy – and I should prefer to make it a fictional one – so that I can illustrate the sort of concern I have about the role of the media in such cases. The setting is real enough and there are enough recent coincidences of fact to make it, I hope, a convincing example.

The Gash Motor Corporation, one of Britain's old-established makers of automobiles, has fallen on hard times. Its cars were good enough for their day, but that was ten years ago. Since then the continental manufacturers and the Japanese have flooded the market with cars which are actually not much better but appeal to the eye more and, unlike the Gash product, bring in a healthy profit for their makers. Gash threaten to close down. Their labour force appeals to the government which, fearing the loss of jobs in an already depressed industrial area, offers large sums of public capital if the corporation will stay in business and retain its workers. Gash, with no great enthusiasm, agrees.

What has the role of the media been, up to this point? It has to be said that after the initial puff given to the Gash models ten years ago, the motoring correspondents have been less and less enthusiastic about them, complaining about their lack of stylishness, their failure to accelerate from 0–60 in under ten seconds (which is actually quite good enough for the average citizen), and their final inability to go more than 90 miles an hour (or 20 mph above the legal speed limit). But, the correspondents point out, such features do appeal to the motoring public, foreign competitors do provide them, and it is not the function of motoring correspondents to give their readers lectures in puritanism.

At the same time, their colleagues, the industrial correspondents, have been logging the story of Gash's deteriorating labour relations. Or *have* they been deteriorating? It depends how far back you look. They are worse this year than they were last, but nothing like as bad as they were fifteen years ago. However, nobody goes that far back. For the fact is, Gash's French, German, Italian and Japanese competitors have only a fraction of the Gash strike rate. They also take half the time, or less, to produce a single car. Gash workers may complain they are low paid, but they are low-productivity as well.

Crisis day dawns with the Gash name hard to sell on any account. Even altering it to G-Cars (standing, claim the cynics, for 'Government Cars') doesn't help. The storm breaks with the state announcing that not only is it refusing to pour any more money into the corporation, but it absolutely forbids the G-Cars management to pay the workers the 33% pay increase they are demanding. On the contrary, G-Cars are required to keep within the 5% guideline which the government has indicated as a voluntary limit. Voluntary in the sense that it is not statutory. 'But', as a senior cabinet minister delicately explains to G-Cars' chairman, Sir Hamilton Gash, 'Just you try breaking it, and your lady-wife may as well sleep on her own for all the use you'll be to her . . .'

So Sir Hamilton offers his workers 4·8%, and the men walk out instantly, even though their (legally unenforceable) agreement has six weeks still to run. Sir Hamilton accuses the men of oath-breaking and poor productivity. The chief shop-steward accuses Sir Hamilton of nit-picking and out-of-date equipment. Before the television cameras, this official declares, 'The men are bitter and frustrated. I have never known them so angry in all my years at this plant. They emphatically reject the cynical attempts of management to hide behind the skirts of the government with their flimsy tale of being obliged to keep to 5%. We'll believe that when we see Sir Hamilton in jail for it. We see no reason why G-Cars should not be given parity with other workers in the industry. The fact that G-Cars are dependent upon public funds imposes a moral obligation upon government to see that parity is achieved – and that means 33% and not a penny less.' *Reporter*: 'But aren't you impressed by the government's argument that a wage increase like that will simply send inflation spiralling up again?' *Shop Steward*: 'We emphatically reject the inflation red herring. If we had been impressed by arguments like that in the past, our wages would have been half what they are today.' *Reporter*: 'But they might have been worth twice as much . . .' *Shop Steward*: 'If you're asking us to put if's and but's before cash on the table, you don't know much about the working man. It's governments that make inflation, not the workers.'

The dispute now develops into a kind of virility contest with Sir Hamilton as the maiden in the middle. The union hastily decides it has no option but to follow its members and bluntly informs the government that '5% is simply not on'. The government pretends not to hear and sends Sir Hamilton a note (which is leaked to the media) reminding him that his contract to supply trucks and buses to the state is liable to instant cancellation. So, under the terms of the government's investment in the corporation, are the jobs of Sir Hamilton and his fellow directors. Ministers of the government are dispatched on speaking tours to every corner of the kingdom, arguing the patriotic case for rigid observance of the 5% limit.

You can fill in the closing chapters of the story according to taste. Fact or fiction, the role of the media in this kind of public controversy follows a standard pattern, a pattern which has produced a standard image of everyone concerned. The workers are selfish, herd-minded, obstinate and ignorant of the wider facts of economic life. We all think we know they are taking home a small fortune every week for doing nothing, though at the time it is widely believed that the Social Security paid to strikers is so generous that it's a wonder they bother to work at all. As for the union, it appears to be run by a pompous juke-box who cares nothing for the nation and keeps repeating 'Totally unacceptable – cash on the table . . .' In any case, he's at the mercy of his shop stewards who are a Trotskyite law unto themselves and constantly ignore the agreements previously reached by the union.

As for management, it is effete and inefficient, remote from its workers and isolated from the technological trends of the industry abroad. There is a class-conscious whiff of the minor public schools about it – it still seems to be interested in knight-hoods – but its increasing subservience to government makes it an object of contempt or even pity rather than active dislike. It becomes increasingly hard to understand why anybody should *want* to go into management.

Government, though, is barely more attractive. Looking back over the past fifteen or twenty years the public, I think, has an image of a leadership that has never been big enough for the job, though it has constantly pretended that it was. Whenever there has been light at the end of the tunnel, it has turned out to be a brief interlude before entering the next tunnel. It only needed an official hymn or two in praise of North Sea oil for everyone to *know* that somehow it would all go wrong and the benefits vanish into the limbo of the national debt without anyone being consciously the better for it. Our politicians never admit to having made a mistake, and yet it seems they have never got anything right. They don't really tell us what they are up to, and when they are asked about it they evade the questions. They are the only leaders we have got, but we no longer expect very much of them. Perhaps that is why the workers have reached the conclusion they should hurry to help themselves.

If this seems a cynical view of our national life, I had better say it is only the view to be distilled from the media and that it is hard to say how widely held it is among ordinary people. A great many of the people I meet and talk to subscribe to it; but I suspect there is a deep stratum I never penetrate where people calmly get on with everyday life in spite of the rumbling overhead; a stratum where, in fact, most people are perfectly happy and don't take the alarms of the articulate too seriously. It may even be that they have developed an immunity to such alarms as a necessary mechanism for survival: for if one took seriously all the shocks and horrors announced by the press and broadcasting, one would shoot oneself in a matter of weeks. But blessed are the meek – who will in fact live to inherit the earth.

I am touching here in my thesis that many of us, especially journalists themselves, take the mass media far too seriously. There is much, much more to life than the front page and the nine o'clock news. It could even be that most of us should go on a diet – ought to cut down our intake of worrying, disturbing news of little or no nutritional value. That is worth bearing in mind, and I shall return to it at the end of this book; but for the moment I must concern myself with those who, for better or worse, are wrapped up in the media and are trying to make out whether they are being served well or ill.

I suppose that a Christian journalist dealing with the story of G-Cars ought to be asking himself where he can see the will of God in it, where he should look for Christian values. But he will have to be careful. For unless he is writing a column of comment and can be quite sure that his readers will recognise it as that, his duty is not to impose what *he* regards as the Christian viewpoint upon them, but to show them the respect of allowing them to make up their minds and to do them the service of supplying the necessary facts and backgrounds.

At this point somebody must be saying, 'But the very selecting of the facts is a form of editorial comment. It might be more honest to make a frankly socialist comment than to make a capitalist selection of the facts and pretend it is objective.' I think this is another case of stretching terms too far. If the choice of facts is a subjective act, then inevitably there is no such thing as objectivity. But if a journalist is consciously striving to be fair, to avoid making a selection according to some loyalty outside the case in hand, then I do not think he can be accused of partisan bias, which is, I believe, the crime against truth. A deliberately socialist or capitalist, Labour, Liberal or Conservative selection of facts in what purports to be 'The News' *is* improper. It may well be that a journalist should take care to recognise his own unconscious prejudices. But it is not a proper substitute for unconscious Conservative bias to substitute a conscious bias towards Labour (or the other way round).

I am writing here, naturally, of media which profess to be objective. Open propaganda, party journals, have the right to be as prejudiced as they please, though I should hope a Christian would feel uncomfortable working on those terms. Media of communication ought to declare their allegiance openly, if they have any; and if they claim to be independent, they should say that too. I would even go to the point of urging that a journalist who is charged with writing straight, factual news ought to foreswear any kind of political party allegiance. One might push on to argue that he should not belong to a trade union, either. I would reject that, on the grounds that if busmen and engineers need a collective, so do journalists who are often much worse paid. But I doubt if their unions should be politically affiliated. It happens that my own union – the National Union of Journalists – is so affiliated; also that no union official has ever ordered me to write to a socialist line. But I still regard the link as unhealthy.

The whole question of union membership among journalists appears to be approaching a crisis, and one which must greatly trouble the Christians among us. I do not wish to sound servile, but neither can I endorse the falsehood that management is always villainous and not to be kept faith with. I have to say therefore, that I find too little regard for serving with honour the employer, the institution, the public to which one has pledged one's word. Throughout journalism there is a growing trend towards the closed shop, towards requiring editors to accept union discipline, and towards the issuing by the union of editorial instructions – for example, on the handling of news to do with race relations, or the 'blacking' of certain sources of news. My personal view is that there are hardly any grounds on which the journalist should strike (political dictation might be one). But this is partly coloured by experience of strike meetings which were more concerned with points of industrial sophistry than with moral principles.

It can certainly be argued that journalists are entitled to protect their working welfare against exploitation. But it seems to me that the more specific this becomes, the wider it opens the way to other forms of exploitation. One is a little tired of hearing that media owners are 'anti-progressive'. The striking thing about the media ownership we have today is not its right wing bias, but how half-heartedly it serves the right. Would the same be true if the left dominated the papers?

I am not so much concerned about the reds in union headquarters. Provided they are constitutionally elected and are honest and able administrators, good luck to them. What worries me is the possibility that a union may take over the individual's responsibility for his own actions, even for his professional judgment. This is a matter of conscience which must concern any Christian, especially a Quaker. For if you regard your work as a form of ministry it must be addressed – over and beyond your employer, your institution and your public – to God our Father. This sort of language may sound pious and unprofessional – not to mention somewhat feudal in the political context, and I should not want the reader to imagine me raising my eyes to heaven before typing a script or entering the studio. Heaven, I think, would be a court of last resort if I could not discern my duty to the rest. But duty and service *are* Christian virtues, and a Christian trade unionist should think very carefully before breaking his contract and disappointing innocent people who depend on his services. I am thinking here not just of viewers and listeners, who may lose little of real value, but also of middlemen like newsagents who are left with nothing to sell when the printers and proprietors go to war with each other.

I do not want to sound naïve about labour relations. I do not deny there is bad management, class warfare, low pay and intolerable working conditions in the world. Some of my friends believe that men of conscience should tackle these first before criticising those who strike against them. Consumers, they argue, care too little about producers. But this seems to me to abdicate our responsibility for the immediate present, which is where we are here and now. We betray the truth if we allow what we *know* to be moral issues – like breaking contracts, leaving hospitals without oxygen, travellers without flights or planes – to slide into a shadowy world of power economics and amorality.

I bring all this into the midst of the saga of G-Cars for a number of reasons. For a start, I fear the day when journalists, as brother unionists, are called upon to demonstrate their solidarity with the supposedly just demands of the G-Cars workers by 'blacking' the management's – and who knows? perhaps even the government's – case. The transporter drivers will have refused to distribute completed cars from the G-Cars works. Why, then, should not journalists refuse to distribute G-Cars' 'anti-worker propaganda aimed at weakening the stand of our brother unionists'? If this line of thought were carried to its logical conclusion, we might see union technicians being ordered to 'pull the plug' on a broadcast by a government minister, the government commanding the broadcasting organisations to carry the speech, police and pickets outside the studios, and transmitters being sabotaged. This scenario need not depend on the political complexion of government or union: it could be justified purely in terms of labour solidarity. But where, or when, does the journalist with a conscience draw the line? It seems to me that it has to be drawn *now*, before it is too late.

When I broadcast something along these lines, one of the letters I received, commenting on it, began, 'Talk about the Tory party at prayer!' But in fact my whole point is that a

Christian journalist ought to be an unreliable partisan, since he should always be searching his conscience for the faults of the side he may feel inclined to favour, and for the redeeming qualities of the one he is inclined to blame. 'Think it possible that you may be mistaken', mistaken, for instance, in accepting convenient labels and stereotypes.

For example, were the motoring correspondents right in dismissing the ten-year-old design – or simply bored? And were they quite uninfluenced by the hospitality lavished on them by foreign manufacturers – the free trips to the Riviera to test-drive the latest models, the generous help with purchasing their own? Did they, perhaps, take an easy ride on the waggon labelled 'I'm knocking Britain!'?

Well, it could have been the other way. Still more generous hospitality from G-Cars might have produced a fraudulent campaign of 'My country right or wrong'. And what is to be said about the productivity issue? The fact is, the media have been exposing it for years. Everybody knows about it, but nobody does anything. Why? To find out would be a real public service.

Newspapers and broadcasting have in fact done their best to supply it. They have suggested lack of capital investment, poor management, restrictive union practices, low work motivation, high boredom, deficient worker participation, negative job satisfaction, historic alienation, fiscal disincentives and just plain idleness. They have also pointed out that Britain, as an industrial power, reached her peak about the period of the Great Exhibition of 1851 and has been in relative decline ever since. What has happened is not really all that surprising: one can almost put it down to exhaustion from so many years of enforced greatness. The trouble is, of course, that while you can make quite an impressive case for the British worker and his dogged refusal to be overworked and underpaid after so many generations – however misrepresented and misunderstood he may be – his foreign counterparts do not have to make any excuses at all: they are busy making motor-cars, and money.

There's no doubting those last facts. But it is, to my mind, a pity that our media don't tell us more about the human reasons behind them. Partly for convenience, partly from repetition, they have fallen into over-simplified patterns of reporting about strikes – routine as football games, resulting in win, lose or draw. They happen because of a pay demand, a dispute over bonus payments, a complaint about shift-working. We seldom hear the precise reasons. The spokesmen for workers and management seldom speak frankly or even intelligibly. Indeed a convention seems to be developing that the management should not speak at all if possible, leaving the platform to the union spokesmen and their just demands for cash on the table. What is extremely difficult, in tightly organised disputes, is for reporters to get direct and revealing conversations with the rank and file. Yet it is extremely important they *should* be on such intimate terms – both with management and men. There are a few notable experts in the business, but generally speaking the journalists sent to cover strikes don't know the plant, don't know the men, don't know the managers and don't understand the problems of any of them from the inside. They would be capable of doing so, given the time and the freedom of movement – but they do not get either. And so the dispute is presented in shorthand terms which can only leave the reader or listener with the conclusion that these are not his fellow men, his brothers, but bloody-minded animals of some sort.

Introduce government and its peculiar modes of expression and evasion, and the air of unreality – of a rather frightening world of inhumans imposed upon our own – settles heavily over the day's news. Yes, the media may well be at fault for their obsessive pursuit of what's called industrial news (meaning strikes), a good deal of which could be left to local rather than national papers and programmes. Yes, they often over-simplify the issues and fail to give them their historic and human background. But the parties involved seldom take the journalists into their confidence, expose to them their real motives, give them the facts. And where government is involved, journalists have learned to watch out for every trick from wishful thinking to downright deception. But I am dealing in my next chapter with relations between journalism and authority.

The chances are that when the G-Cars dispute is settled, very little will have been learnt because nobody will be quite sure what has happened, because nobody has come clean or believed that anybody else has. And this, alas, shadows the role of the media in every public controversy. There is little to suggest that the media *do* play a particularly creative role in such controversies – creative in the sense of helping to lead and articulate the great mass of public opinion. I have painted a picture of the media as bridges over which journalists carry messages; but I have to say that the messages are largely one-way. People in authority express themselves to the public, but the public says very little in return. Listening to one another, the communicators – the decision makers – may come to the conclusion that opinion has moved their way. The next election may demonstrate a certain acquiescence, but if one takes an issue like capital punishment, nationalisation or immigration one is liable to find a very different result by way of a public opinion poll.

I am bound to end on a rather a pessimistic note. A Quaker's ultimate faith rests in the Light Within, and I suppose that if it gives him a prophetic insight into events he will pursue where it leads and tell what he sees by it. But, at the risk of repeating myself, events can be enormously complicated and sweeping prophecy is liable to generate more heat than light. The Christian journalist should content himself with chipping away, conscientiously, at the fragment of truth embedded in the rock before him. The grand design will be for others to discern.

7.   Scribes and Pharisees

Foremost among those who belive they do know, and can indeed control, the grand design are the politicians. If you have a conditioned reflex to that word, I suppose it is largely the fault of the media. It is we scribes who have presented them as pharisees: exclusive, self-righteous, hypocritical, the sole vehicles of power and truth in their own estimation. But if they do seem that way, may it not be the demands and attentions of journalists which have made them so? Have we perhaps exposed them to so searching a light that they dare not behave any more like human beings? As this book proceeds, I detect a sort of howl-back phenomenon, such as you get when a microphone picks up the sound from a loudspeaker it is feeding, passes it back, picks it up again, round and round until an intolerable howl builds up. In the same way I suspect the media may report something *of* the world *to* the world, report the world's reactions to that back to the world again, and its reactions to that and to that and to that until the original event has multiplied itself to the power of *n*. Just so, when journalists report on a politician they are, to some degree, reporting on their own creation and on his reaction to their reports. Whoever may be unimpressed by the work of the journalists, politicians are always among their most avid students.

It is, I suspect, the attention of the media as much as anything which has led to the present intolerable overworking of MPs. There is far too much legislation because governments are expected to be 'doing something' all the time. The media are constantly exposing things that are wrong, ministers constantly leap to the dispatch box to announce laws to rectify them. MPs are led to feel guilty if they are not seen to be working harder than most of their constituents, though in fact they would be more in touch with those constituents if they spent more of their time outside the House. But to be a part-timer is deemed to be unprofessional and somehow dishonourable. The media prefer the full time politician, always available, even on the Sabbath day of rest.

This is not really the place for a critique of Westminster democracy, but some analysis is inevitable when we are discussing the subtle relationship between government and media. Journalists have no official standing in the system at all. They have no inalienable right to report debates in the Commons and none whatever to question ministers, let alone civil servants. The Constitution of the United States forbids any abridgement of the Freedom of the Press, and that Amendment has been steadily extended until today in America there is in effect a 'Right to Know' unless the State can demonstrate otherwise. No such right exists in Britain. The access of the media to what is happening behind the doors of state is limited by all kinds of restrictions ranging from the Official Secrets Act to the doctrine of *sub judice* and the Privilege of the House, to old fashioned prejudice against the press.

But why *should* journalists have any right to know? *1*) Who elected them? *2*) Why should they be trusted? *3*) How could government get on with running the country? *4*) How could any minister or civil servant speak frankly if what he said, perhaps in an early stage of discussion, was liable to be splashed over the front pages?

The first question I have touched on already. It is one for which the journalists should have a swift answer by now. It is easy enough to point out to the average politician that his constituents didn't get a lot of choice when they elected *him*, seeing that most candidates are presented by their parties on a take him or leave him basis. In a low poll an MP may be elected by the votes of a quarter or less of the registered constituents. A political correspondent might at least claim the support of the quarter million or more readers who buy his paper. Nor is it true to say he is self-appointed. For the chances are he won his job on the basis of performance and in the face of stiff competition. Moreover a delinquent correspondent can be overthrown

97

and replaced a great deal more swiftly than a delinquent or incompetent MP.

Even so, I don't find that a very satisfactory argument. In the end I believe a reporter who is asked by what right he pokes his nose into government can only answer: by no right, as our laws stand – but by vocation. How representative is he? He is not there to represent: he is there to serve, to serve his editor, his paper, his public and – if he believes his work to be sacramental, as I do – his God over all.

> Who sweeps a room as for thy laws,
> Makes that and the action fine

wrote Cowper, and that goes for the divine drudgery of political reporting. If it sounds pompous to speak of serving the truth, I'm sorry, but that is what most of the profession are trying to do, each after his own light. It is not, I think, an ignoble occupation.

Why should journalists be trusted by politicians? The simplest answer to this is, 'You need us. We need *each other*.' For in spite of what I said earlier about journalists having over-stretched politicians, it would be quite wrong to suppose that politicians are innocent and unwilling victims of the media machine. Most politicians know – or think they know – perfectly well how to use the media. That use may be entirely legitimate, like bringing to public attention the availability of some new pension, or it may be fatuous self-advertisement, after the style of, 'I call upon the Minister for a *full-scale enquiry* into the scandal of noisy seagulls which are making a nightmare of working people's seaside holidays.'

Nevertheless, politicians are torn by doubts about the media. On the one hand they *want* the publicity; on the other hand they *don't*. The fact is, they want the right publicity, not the wrong publicity (right and wrong being defined by the subject himself). A minister of the late administration of Northern Ireland once said to me at a lunch, 'If only the government could take responsibility to put out a daily bulletin of the facts as it alone knows them ...' 'There's one already,' I reminded him, 'and they call it *Pravda*.' There is no way I know of enjoying the advantages of a free press without the disadvantages. Did I hear laughter at the word free? At least let us not pretend it is in chains, as some are. Our press is a great deal freer than most, and I don't believe that making it a kind of social service or even a public corporation like the BBC would bring it any nearer the ideal.

In the end, politicians should trust journalists because there is really no alternative. As we have seen increasingly of late, most secrets come out in the end, and they seldom look better for being held back. Nonetheless, journalists have a very good record of keeping confidences: it is not in the reporter's interests to alienate his sources, nor is it in the politician's to deceive his messenger. In this exchange, however, the politician has the advantage: if he is of any eminence he can do without a particular reporter more easily than the reporter can do without him. Correspondents are sometimes obliged to return to a tainted well.

I can see very few cases for secrecy: defence secrets if you believe in them (I don't), short-term police tactics, some diplomacy where delicate timing is called for. Otherwise, if truth is to make us free, we must surely press on towards open government. People have a right to conduct their private affairs in private, and I hold no brief for intrusion into privacy. But I see no reason why public affairs, commissioned and paid for by the public, should be protected as if they were private property.

I can understand that some people have a psychological objection to working with strangers looking over their shoulders (though I sometimes suspect that is due to their own doubts about what they are doing). But it is not seriously proposed that reporters should be able to prowl the offices of Whitehall, rummaging through civil servants' desks. It is a question of allowing serious, qualified, accredited correspondents to make their contacts and conduct their enquiries without being obstructed and spoon-fed by inappropriately named Information Officers. Why should we not know, for example, what alternatives are in draft for the route of the new motorway, what dates are being considered for the elections, what names are on the short-list for the Royal Commission, what were the arguments in Cabinet for and against withdrawing troops from Ulster? Why should we not know these things before it is too late – seriously, why not?

The classic explanation is that such openness would damage the anonymous objectivity of the civil service and introduce partisan divisions where none at present exist; that it would destroy the fiction of the collective responsibility of Cabinet; and that it would encourage ministers and civil servants alike to strike poses, play to the gallery or to influential interests. 'Ministers have to be quite insincere enough in the House,' I have been told, 'for goodness sake allow then to let their hair down in the secrecy of Cabinet.'

It is all a sad reflection on the gap between private and public candour. From time to time over the years I have watched the House of Commons in action, without ever getting used to this – to the sturdily maintained pretence that *my* side is totally right, *your* side totally wrong. One knows it is a pretence, because one meets members in private afterwards and they say, 'I'm afraid we've fouled this business up – the opposition is perfectly right', or, it may be, 'That was a brilliant performance by the government – we haven't really a leg to stand on.' I have heard members talk like that to each other, knowing they were in the presence of a reporter, and knowing, too, that by convention they would not be quoted. I am not suggesting that confidence should be systematically violated, but I think it a pity there is such a need for it.

Am I naïve? Again I am told the pretence of infallibility is necessary for party morale and discipline. You could not, it is argued, keep a party together if members were liable to jump up and confess their official policy was wrong. At that rate you would soon find government and opposition back-benchers walking into the same lobby together, and stable government would collapse. Telling the truth in public may *sound* very Christian, but in fact (I was told) it is shot full of the sin of pride. Who is the individual member to say that he knows best, has a private hot-line to the angel of truth, or to claim the right to overthrow a whole government by his single casting vote?

All of which, it seems to me, throws an interesting light on what the Westminster system actually does, rather than what it is thought to do. It does not necessarily provide representative or even responsive government, so much as maintain in office the leadership of whichever party has, under the rules, secured the next term. What that party then does depends more upon its internal balances and influences than on what the country is thought to want or need (which is largely unknowable). If this is so, it seems to me better to admit it frankly than to allow one's readers or listeners to assume that the speeches they hear reflect a representative, rather than plebiscitary, democracy.

Am I preaching cynicism? No, and for two reasons: the first, that realism about human nature has always been fundamental to Christian understanding; and the second, that it would be wrong to assume that the human beings involved are necessarily corrupt. British politicians very rarely are, and the inscrutability of the British floating vote makes it very difficult for a party leader to assume that he is bound to stay in power and so can indulge in any enormities he fancies. The British political leader is generally a sincere and dedicated man; sincere in that he genuinely believes in the ability of politics to make life better, and dedicated in that he hopes to serve his people through politics. Insofar as he wants power, he wants it to do good with, and in this way he may be a better Christian, a better servant of the children of God, than a carping, cavilling journalist. When it comes to doing good, achieving anything positive that can be pointed to, the journalist will have very little to show on the Day of Judgement: far less, for example, than the lowliest parish priest or a conscientious back-bencher who has tended his constituency clinic.

Who am I, for example, to sneer at our post-war prime ministers for landing us in today's mess? Have I really tried to understand their difficulties? Have I given them credit for what they have achieved, for the sacrifices they have made of their health and happiness? And what, if anything, did I do to make their burdens any lighter?

I believe that a Christian journalist should err on the side of generosity when assessing a politician; and yet, and *yet* I remember an injunction about being wise as serpents. One has been charmed, misled and downright lied to too often over the years to let one's guard down. Gullibility is not good quality for a journalist; it provides a poor service to his readers in the long run.

And so, with all the sympathy in the world, the reporter finds himself conducting the challenging interview. Often he gets letters afterwards denouncing him for his rudeness and impertinence (though no politician brought up in the House of Commons is likely to bruise easily or be thrown by an unexpected question). What the reporter should write in reply is that he is obliged to represent the opposition – the other side of the case that is not represented in the studio, and those thousands of listeners who probably did *not* write in to describe how they sat at home muttering, 'But what about *this*? Go on and ask him *that*!'

It is hardly surprising the relationship between journalist and politician is occasionally shadowed with ill-feeling. As MacNeice wrote, 'None of our hearts is pure, we always have mixed motives', but no one enjoys being reminded of that in public. Nevertheless the relationship is more cordial than the public might suppose. At times it even becomes *too* cordial, so that things are not published that probably ought to be published, for fear of hurting an old friend. The gulf between political journalist and politician remains, but it is a narrow one and quite a number of journalists yield to the temptation to cross over.

Some pages earlier I asked how could government get on with running the country if it had to expose its operations more fully to the media? I don't honestly think it would make much difference, except that projects would be more thoroughly prepared before they came to the parliamentary process, instead of being fought over lengthily in both houses. But behind the question there lies the proud assumption – one that spills over into my final question about frankness – that government knows best and ought to be trusted. Should not a journalist who believes in rendering unto Caesar the things that are Caesar's, accept that?

It may sound odd after so much scepticism, but let me put it

102

another, more plausible way. What has all this to do with Christianity anyway? Shouldn't religion and politics stay well apart, and a book like this turn to more spiritual matters than how to reform Whitehall?

It is my experience that people who demand that the churches should stay out of politics usually mean that the churches should tacitly endorse their own particular party. In fact the churches have always been in politics, up to their necks, and it seems to me that the real essential is not to award holiness to any single party but to see to it that there are Christians infecting all of them.

The theologian Hans Küng, whose book *On being a Christian* stands next to my Bible, tells us that almost the only message Christianity has for politics is one that politicians would rather not hear: that we should not hesitate to make unilateral concessions to our adversaries without thought of our own advantage. It is no shame, thinks Küng, for a man in authority *not* to exploit his power to the full, and no disgrace for leadership to serve others rather than dominate them, or to give away power, profit and influence. One should be very cautious, Küng believes, of claiming Christian authority for any policy for which there is not a very clear mandate in scripture.

It is clear enough to me that Jesus himself was no politician or freedom-fighter, though he did not scorn men of action – not even centurions and tax-gatherers. His concern was that people in all walks of life should take to heart his message of love, forgiveness and the relative unimportance of worldly reward and achievement. He asserted the importance of the poor, he depreciated the values of the rich, but beyond that I can see no reason why a Christian should be a Socialist rather than a Conservative and every reason why a Christian should make a poor dogmatist in any party. I have suggested that if there is one instinct the Christian journalist should have it is a disinclination to accept stereotypes or to join in the denigration of popular scapegoats; and the same should apply, surely, to the Christian politician.

It also occurs to me that if we truly believe in the fatherhood and guardianship of God over us all, we ought to take a generally optimistic view of affairs, reluctant to cry havoc and confident that the hand of God is to be found somewhere in everything, and that even disaster, even the shaking of our foundations, may be his opportunity for resurrection and renewal.

Which is why, to get back to the question of frankness and openness in public affairs, it might be no bad thing for our political system to submit itself to the shock of drawing back the curtains that hide its proceedings not only from the public but even from itself. Anyone who has gone through the ordeal of analysis knows the agony of disentangling one's own distortions, evasions and self-justifications and emerging into honesty. It might be the same with a political system that adopted truly open government. What, after all, has it got to hide?

One thing it has been hiding for many years is what Westminster knows as the lobby system, under which specialist correspondents receive regular briefings from the departments they cover, but commonly on the understanding that they may not say in their reports where their information came from. That is what lies behind those mysterious items declaring out of the blue, 'Britain is to take an important new initiative towards settling the South Africa crisis . . .', or 'Whitehall expects the Minister of Agriculture to outlaw Russian potatoes. . . .' A milder form of the practice lies behind those stories from Washington beginning, 'Sources high in the administration revealed today . . .', or 'Officials who declined to be identified. . . .' The object in both cases is to transmit more or less dubious propaganda for which the speaker cannot afterwards be blamed because, in theory, he never really existed. And it has the attraction from the journalist's point of view of adding a pinch of mystery to the dishes he serves up – a hint of the second sight or at least of friends in high places.

Efforts have been made, and have failed, to break the pernicious system. From time to time ministers announce they are abandoning it, but always it creeps back. For one thing, it enables ministers to feed their titbits only to selected and trusted reporters. Since the lobby meetings do not officially take place, it is impossible for outsiders to demand admission to them. Further, it enables ministers to use the media without violating the convention that Parliament must be first to hear any official tidings. Should it not be the first? Certainly it should where there is good reason. But when a leak is part of the ploy, it is better that it should be open and reliable. To those who fear that openness would lead to ministers waging propaganda wars against each other, the answer is, surely, that they do so already and that exposing such wars to the public would at least give the public some chance to suggest how they ought to be resolved – even by knocking the combatants' heads together or getting a new government.

As things are, it is debatable whether the media are doing a better job on behalf of the public or on behalf of the politicians who use them to communicate. A White House official once told Robert MacNeil, the Canadian news anchorman, that television was not only the most powerful of the mass media but also the most subservient and weak-kneed, the most susceptible to official pressure. The fact is, says MacNeil, 'TV wants to stay out of trouble.'

That is certainly true of television and broadcasting in general on our own side of the Atlantic. This is not only because European broadcasting is much more dependent on the state for its licensing and finance, but because it has a certain guilt complex about itself. Perhaps we *do* sensationalise, trivialise, spread violence and immorality. Perhaps we *don't* give the politicians a fair deal or produce as much moral uplift as we should. And worst of all, perhaps we *are* usurpers of the power properly confided to the elected. All of this we begin to fear, and so we seek to appease those who accuse us.

One way we do this is by, in effect, castrating ourselves. The argument is that since broadcasting is so powerful, and since in a liberal democracy we do not wish to surrender its power totally to government, it won't take a stand on controversial matters at all. Even if they have investigated an issue thoroughly and arrived at a definite conclusion about it, the broadcasters will not stand up and declare, 'I accuse!' They will invite somebody *pro* and somebody *con* and encourage them to neutralise each other's arguments – which, if they are experienced Members of Parliament, they will do with no trouble at all. Nobody can then complain that his point of view has not been represented fairly, and if there are no letters of protest within a week, everybody concerned can sigh with relief and move on. The great power of broadcasting has been exerted in equal and opposite directions, so that if any movement does take place, at least broadcasting cannot be blamed.

I have established already, I hope, that I am profoundly sceptical of the supposed power of broadcasting. Analogies with the demonstrated power of TV commercials do not impress me, for nobody sells violence or fornication or socialism the way they sell petrol or furniture polish or teabags. And why, seeing there is so much sport on television, isn't everyone out playing games? No, the true influences are elsewhere. I suspect that broadcasting actually offers more controversy about topical issues than people really want. What they really want, if I may be forgiven a sweeping generalisation, is entertainment and escape, not intellectual stimulation. And I cannot honestly blame them for that, nor find it morally wrong or spiritually un-Christian of people working in the media to minister to those needs rather than pursuing my own disturbing ministry of information and enlightenment. Am I really serving Jack Trevaskiss, commuting bank clerk, better by providing him with a description of Pope Paul's lying-in-state than the photographer who took that heart-lifting nude on page 3 of his *Sun*? The theology of the pin-up deserves closer study.

I am convinced that the main reason why politicians and civil servants are far more suspicious of broadcasting than they are of the press is that they genuinely believe that the electronic media have a stronger magic than the printed word. I use the word *magic* with some care, because it seems to me there really is an element of the supernatural in this belief. We can all understand how printing is carried out. In the primitive form of a rubber stamp, we can all do it. But broadcasting, like flying, defies common sense, no matter how carefully the physics and electronics are explained to us. We know that the real people are miles away in some studio, or even in bed by now, while the tape recording rolls through; and yet they appear to be speaking to us, looking at us, in our own home here and now. And this illusion of reality adds danger. Because we can see it and hear it we are virtually witnessing it – it must be so 'for the camera cannot lie'. Yet we know that the cameraman and the film editor can. I have done the exercise of taking a camera down one side of a street, selecting the shots to make it look cheerful and well-kept. Then back up the other side, only filming the angles that will make the same street appear rundown and sinister. Background music completes the transformation.

The medium, then, is only as reliable as the person using it. And yet it is curious that the medium of broadcasting is still treated as something dangerous in itself, to be licensed and controlled like alcohol. The same journalist can say something in print and be totally ignored – then repeat it in a broadcast and create uproar. You have to be a broadcaster to realise how sensitive people can be to views they do not share. There is something about having a stranger use this 'official' or 'pontifical' medium to introduce into your home ideas you do not wish to receive, which you, the listener or viewer, find doubly offensive, even threatening. The Christian broadcaster ought, in charity, to bear this in mind and say what he has to say with humility and readiness to receive correction.

The journalist and the politician, the scribe and the pharisee, circle round each other, tails a-quiver like bottom-sniffing dogs. I need not describe all the other antics they perform, for their mutual fascination knows no bounds. The journalist is fascinated by power, the politician by communication, and neither can do without the other, which he lacks. The politician is convinced that he is not inspired by mere personal ambition, that he stands for principles far greater than himself. But the journalist knows that – except for a few enthusiasts – those principles are meaningless to most of his public, that they can only be communicated in terms of personality. And so he personalises his story, presenting it in terms of human drama or comedy, to the fury of the politician. 'Let's stick to the issues', is the cry of the party leaders at elections; 'Stop cashing in on personalities!'

Yet is the journalist so far wrong? After all, the British

107

political system is, or was, based on the theory of ministerial responsibility; and when the election is over and the manifestos put away, what is left is personality confronting the inscrutable future. Isn't it really more important to be sure of a Prime Minister's courage, his judgment of his fellows, his compassion, than his theories of how many houses can be built, what farmers should get for potatoes and what level of inflation should be expected in two years' time? All of those things will be as they will be, no doubt: what the voter can help to decide is, what sort of people shall have the authority to cope with them. And the journalist has a unique opportunity to present and test those people, as personalities. And this, I submit, is the proper Christian approach.

I have said that I don't much care for the set-piece interview. I don't care much, either, for the groomed and packaged address to camera. It is precisely for such that the professional image-makers and candidate-packagers are hired. I question whether they have had much success: you might say they sold Richard Nixon to the American people (though I think the feebleness of the opposition was what really lost the day) – but if so, they failed to prevent Nixon betraying himself on television when the Watergate scandal broke. In any case, there are few places more unnatural and less likely to reveal a man as he really is than a radio or television studio.

So once again we come back to the journalist, to the reporter himself, as the messenger who must convey to his public the feeling of *What it is like*, or in this case *What he is like*, an impression he can only get by following his subject through the day, meeting him in various places and circumstances until he sees him in the round. A patient television reporter with an unobtrusive camera crew can do this, allowed the time and the money. It can only be done successfully, of course, given the subject's co-operation, given a certain surrender of his private life. It has been my experience, as a television reporter, that such a surrender is well worthwhile. Good people come across honestly as what they are, though shifty folk reveal themselves in their deceptions. The responsibility of the reporter who is trying to interpret character like this is a heavy one. But then his own reputation, his own character, is also at stake in the making of the programme.

On rare occasions, the probing reporter finds himself confronting a 'Keep Out' sign: *Publication not in the National Interest – Security – Sub Judice*. What he has to decide here is whether it is genuinely in the interests of the *nation* that something should be suppressed or only in the interests of a party or a government. The two are by no means the same, though they are often draped with the same patriotic emblems. We have already noted some celebrated cases, like Suez and Watergate, where every resource of the state was deployed to enforce secrecy. That they were all concealed for so long demonstrates the power of authority (especially British authority) to hush things up. That they were eventually disclosed and hypocrisy dispelled is a tribute to the diligence of the reporter. And it is surely better that the deception should be unmasked by the guilty nation's own reporters rather than by the propogandists of an adversary. That is a choice that critics of investigative reporting should contemplate: would you rather have the nation's dirty linen washed in the *Sunday Times* or in *Pravda*?

The mass media have good reason to take what authority offers with some caution. Yet face-to-face, those in authority are usually as agreeable as one could wish to meet. You cannot help sympathising with them for the impossible tasks they are set. It is galling for them to hear their problems misunderstood by the media – and yet fear of admitting their own limitations inhibits them from admitting frankly what the true dimensions of those problems are. I have no doubt, myself, that every institution – government, business, church – would be healthier, happier and in the end more successful if it threw its affairs wide open and talked about them freely. Journalists and public would be better informed, and no longer could two rumours and a half-denial be assembled to make a fully blown scandal. As things are, it is easy to say that the media should publish the truth. But how can we publish it if those who know it won't tell it?

8. Publish and be Blessed

A journalist dealing with religious affairs, as I do, gets an unusual perspective on human hopes and fears as reflected by the mass media. On the one hand, an impatient assumption that atheism is normal and that only the elderly or insecure need faith; on the other, a deep longing for warmth and reassurance. On the one hand, a demand for what are known in the trade as 'batty vicar stories', on the other, a fascination with holy relics and the supernatural.

My mind goes back once more to those days spent in St Peter's Square. What went we out for to see? A prophet, we hoped, and perhaps more than a prophet. At least a messenger of hope and certainty, telling the world quite simply that there was indeed a heavenly Father that loved it and cared for it and had a purpose for it. I am not sure whether we heard such a message, but I was acutely aware of the world's longing for it. You might say I was waiting for good news – even *the* good news; though I doubt if my editor would have been much impressed if I had telephoned him with the announcement, 'Jesus Loves Us'.

One reason why, for me, the moral dilemmas of journalism remain largely unresolved is the apparent impossibility of conveying that, the greatest of all good news, within the definitions of news as Broadcasting House and Fleet Street know it. What is a Christian, who believes in the good news of the Gospel, doing in a profession which seems to depend upon bad news? I argued at the beginning of this book that it is not, in fact, all bad news, and I insist as firmly as ever that ministering to the truth is a worthy occupation for any Christian. What the truth is may be far from easily come by, but I went on to explain my vocation in Quaker terms, defending mass communication as being a good deal less destructive than mass conflict.

I believe that firmly. But the world of news around me may seem to offer very little encouragement. I am glad not to be alone in the struggle to communicate. John Whale, once my friendly opposition in Washington, wrote long before I ever did of the journalist's duty to resist the retreat from reason as language became discredited, specialised, 'furred by advertising' as he put it. And Robert MacNeil, a former colleague in television, has written of how the convention of impersonal newscasting can oblige a correspondent to present as true what he actually knows to be false – but cannot say so.

I find myself wondering sometimes whether we should not all be better off with less literacy, less communication? Would people really be any the more likely to succumb to evil counsel, false prophets? But it is foolish to imagine the clock can be put back. Mass communication is here to stay, and most of the time it does have useful information to offer, it does help people to keep an eye on their rulers, it does provide them with daily diversions from life's tedium and stress.

I believe that the mass media more often under-estimate than over-estimate the intelligence of their public. Nevertheless, what you and I may deplore in today's media may be precisely what most people like about them. You and I may demand a record of truth and high morality; but somewhere along the line, somebody has to see it as a business proposition. The sort of paper you and I would really like – a paper with no advertisements at all, with copious and literate dispatches from far-flung correspondents, and beautiful landscapes superbly photographed – that is the sort of paper nobody could afford.

The difficulty is to explain to high-minded people how difficult, how very nearly impossible, the production of a newspaper or a newscast is, never mind what the contents. The actual writing of it takes less time than one would wish: so much of the rest is logistics and labour relations.

Strangely, too, nobody knows what it is the public really wants of the media. But there is usually no doubt what one's editor wants and so – since he is in power – his word is my command.

Here is another element in the dilemma. From some points of view a newspaper or a news programme is a team effort. That is one of its joys. Just as playing in an orchestra carries you along, so working as part of a news team, being one of the boys, is satisfying and invigorating in itself. The team is proud of its professionalism, of knowing how to achieve the impossible. It shows off to itself, cares more for its own opinion of itself than for any outside opinion. And so it may come to forget the public for which it is meant to be working.

This team spirit endangers another basic value. When you examine a front page or a news programme closely, you find that it breaks down into a collection of individual contributions, each of which was once the responsibility of a single reporter or cameraman. It was up to him to assess the situation and decide what to report or to film and what to ignore. Ideally there is nothing between these witnesses who are giving evidence and the public who are hearing it. Yet every reporter is more or less at the mercy of a sub-editor who may cut or rewrite what he has written, and every cameraman is at the mercy of the processing and cutting rooms. Over the years a journalist gets used to seeing his work emerge at the far end of the line looking rather different from what he originally had in mind. Often that is inevitable, sometimes an improvement, but it seems to me there is something morally uncomfortable about the way responsibility is subdivided.

To me journalism is essentially something that an individual does and for which he alone can take responsibility. He must investigate his story and then report what impression it has made upon him. So I am opposed to the collectivisation of journalism in any way, and to any attempt to standardise attitudes and insights. It seems to me that if a reporter is biased, his readers will have the wit to find him out, and if he is outrageously wrong he can be sacked. But collective journalism, whether enforced by party policy or union rule will never admit to being wrong and cannot easily be dislodged once it has seized power. That is why I dread schemes for democratic or participatory editing. I may be condemned as 'elitist', but the sobering truth about an elite is that it is chosen on merit and must then assume the responsibility for what it does. It is also required to labour until it drops. The point about the parable of the talents is that we are expected to exploit to the utmost those talents that we have. The dilemma looming ahead in contemporary journalism is: will one be able to exercise such responsibility for oneself, or will it be taken out of the individual's hands?

Earlier I mentioned that the problem of truth in journalism often lay beyond the mere facts. Often it consists in determining at what level the truth of a given story lies. Has the reporter found the truth when he writes, 'Three children were burnt to death in a basement flat in Camden Town today while their parents were out at work?' Barely. He would go on to find out how the fire started, why the parents had left the children alone, why nobody rescued them. The reporter might end up with a story taking us back to the arrival of a refugee family from Uganda, unable to speak English or to understand what help was available to it, forced to accept wages so low that both parents were obliged to work long hours to support their children. That would be nearer 'the truth' than the bare facts of the children's death and it might even produce constructive action.

To their credit, journalists are, in fact, unearthing that kind of truth every day. You may find it, perhaps, more readily in local newspapers and broadcasting than in the national media, and journalists are not always loved for it by those in authority. In the days when I presented a nightly news programme we had an unofficial motto: 'We hope this is the truth. We're sure it isn't the whole truth. It'll be a miracle if it's nothing but the truth.' What we did not say – and rightly – was: 'Since we can't be absolutely sure of the truth, we'll say nothing.'

I believe that although we may never arrive at the central core of the truth, we must never foreclose on it or assume that the little progress we can make towards it is not worthwhile.

One of the most tantalising dilemmas presented by journalism involves the choice between accuracy and attractiveness, between reflecting the truth in all its forbidding complexity on

113

the one hand and getting it over to the largest possible audience on the other. The more you know about a situation, the less straightforward it becomes: the more fascinating, perhaps, and yet the harder to explain in simple terms. There are times when I am tempted to cry, 'Don't confuse me with any more facts just as I'm beginning to understand it!' And yet the journalist prides himself on, and is paid for, explaining any situation to almost anyone. And it is this which leads him into the sin of over-simplification. He takes pleasure in communicating; he longs to know that he has been understood; and in striving towards that he yields too often to the temptation to throw half of his message away and deliver a caricature of the original.

This leads on to a further dilemma: are we in journalism really informing people, as we like to claim, or merely entertaining them? To a certain extent we *must* entertain or nobody will hear us. Writers and broadcasters, since they cannot pretend to be showing literally what happened, are in the nature of abstract artists: they have to present things symbolically, impressionistically. Writers can be re-read if their message does not register immediately. But radio broadcasters, since they are not physically present to reinforce their words with gestures and expressions, must often overact in order to squeeze their experience down through the microphone and even drag the listener back up the wire to join in the experience. Is there too much histrionics, I wonder, or too little? How far should one care about whether one's message is being received and understood? Or should one simply dump it on the doorstep with a 'Take it or leave it!'? The best journalism, it seems to me, has something in common with poetry: its compression, its rhythm, its evocative use of language to draw the listener in, its treatment of language as if it were a sacrament. For language, after all, was not accounted too poor an instrument for the Son of God to use.

And yet even as I write those words, I fancy I can hear my first chief sub-editor – a sadistic Scot – being noisily sick in his wastepaper basket.

I am taking, it seems, a highly subjective view of journalism and claiming it is a Christian one . Americans, I find, often

114

express horror at the mixing of personal views with factual reporting in English journalism. The point can be demonstrated by comparing a piece of fact-packed American agency prose ('Britain's five-foot-four-inch 52-year-old German-descended monarch Elizabeth the Second ...') with, say, Robert Fisk reporting to the *Times* from the civil war in Beirut. He remarks how the Christian militia are so 'cock-a-hoop at their ability to withstand Syrian firepower that the essential ingredient for the success of any talks – the desire of the encircled minority for an end to the fighting – simply does not exist'. This sentence contains assertions of opinion that could well be challenged. But to the able and experienced Fisk they are as good as fact; they explain and illuminate the situation for us; and we who have learnt to trust the *Times* and Fisk over the years are grateful for them.

I would dare to say it is the objective, factual style of the agency reporter which has allowed horrors like the Vietnam War and Northern Ireland troubles to become routine and drag on. It is only when the creative reporter experiences and expresses the event fairly but caringly – recognising that it involves God's children, his brothers and sisters, and not two-dimensional objects – that his readers begin to realise that this is *not* just part of the remote news world.

This has its meaning for the consumers as well as the creators of the media: that careful discrimination between papers, programmes and reporters is as necessary as it is between brewers or butchers or car-makers. And, by and large, you will get what you pay for.

Unfortunately what you will get in a good many cases *is* a world of sex, crime and triviality. Am I still in no sort of moral dilemma over that? How can I defend the freedom of the press to publish that sort of rubbish?

I must start by declining to take quite so disastrous a view of things as Mr Muggeridge and Mrs Whitehouse do. And personally, as a Religious Affairs correspondent, I think I can plead not guilty to any charge of publishing sex, crime and trivia. Restrictive laws can be passed if Parliament thinks we need them, though I should defend the right of conscientious resistance, provided the resistor took the consequences.

I am not really shocked that the popular media don't operate according to strictly Christian moral standards – nor do I think they can be made to, for this is no longer a strictly Christian society. I am shocked, however, that our secular society, in which the media stand rooted, should have evolved a public education system that produces so little respect for education, or for scholarly, cultural or artistic excellence of any kind. Shocked, too, that the church should have lost its grip upon morality, culture and education.

If this is the post-Christian society we can't assume that the moral seriousness of yesterday's Sunday-school teachers is shared by today's media people. But I am surprised that churches, PTAs, families and individuals don't use their own powers of communication more intelligently. I have little use for those who appoint themselves spokesmen for pressure-groups that turn out to have almost no members, but I have to say that readers, viewers and listeners under-estimate their potential influence. It would be nice if they wrote in as readily with praise as with blame, but either way their communications have a much greater effect (in my experience) than those who send them realise. To command respect such messages need to be well-informed and couched in reasonable terms. Tactically it is better to address them to a known individual – a reporter or producer – rather than to some nameless editor or director-general. And I can assure you it concentrates the broadcaster's mind wonderfully to know that an entire diocesan synod or bench of elders considers his talk last Saturday to have been 'grossly unfair to the traditions of our church'.

One way the media have devised of processing such complaints is to set up a self-policing organisation like the Press Council. Every year some 700 readers do complain to it, though far less than one in ten has his complaint upheld. I don't much care for the system myself, partly because it encourages what I see as the exaggeration of the media's influence. On the other hand, I do believe that the media are slippery and often ungenerous about confessing their errors. They would earn

116

greater goodwill and lose little face if they apologised more often and more graciously. The laws of England are oppressive enough when it comes to libel, slander, official secrets and *sub judice*: it should be possible to prosecute for any serious injury, while trivial affronts are best ignored. I find it hard to justify the half-way house of the Press Council, which shows an unbecoming tendency, at times, to assume that the duty of the press is to uplift public morals instead of reporting them as they are.

One of my strongest regrets as a communicator is that the communication remains so much in one direction. I talk a good deal, I make a sudden sally with microphone or notebook, but how much time do I spend listening to people outside the magic circle of the newsmakers? I am constantly telling people what they are supposed to want to know, but what evidence is there that they do? What good does this derivative, parasitical job do? Less, perhaps, than becoming an honest carpenter and spending regular evenings with my wife and children; for journalism, like politics, is a terrible devourer of family life.

And yet perhaps this is the sin of depreciating the talents one has been granted. On the one hand the perils of pride, on the other those of false humility used as an excuse for sloth. Maybe our Lord did begin as a carpenter; but – *pace* Malcolm Muggeridge – his public relations devices and his press conferences produced some of the finest journalism – the Gospels – that the world knows.

No journalist would admit publicly that his job was anything but sheer hell. But the fact is, one would not stay with it if it did not bring occasional glimpses of heaven. The very transitoriness of everything one does is satisfying. You exhaust yourself, even risk your life, to fill a minute or two of time on the air, and then it is gone, forgotten, blown away. It wasn't all that good anyway, you tell yourself: I'll do better next time. And so – on to the next dragonfly drama! Louis Heren of the *Times* compares getting rid of a story to passing a good motion (though he uses a briefer expression). I know exactly what he means. There's a relief in throwing away the day's clutter of facts and quotes, even a certain glory in sacrificing one's prose on the altar of a deadline. Journalists commonly yearn for the immortality of a book between covers. Broadcasters can't even brood over their words in a back-numbers file. But perhaps it is the very evanescence that prevents us from taking ourselves too seriously. I am not sure it is quite the same as the Christian virtue of humility, but at any rate it is very hard for a journalist to deceive himself that his work belongs to all the ages.

I believe that every Christian should be able to look upon his work as his vocation: something that he is uniquely called to do for the greater glory of God and for the service of God's children, his own brothers and sisters. In that sense I can regard my journalism as a vocation, even a sacred ministry. Nevertheless I sometimes wonder if it has not become what Ivan Illich might call a disabling profession, so organised as actually to *obstruct* communication, obscure meaning, prevent understanding, by insisting that it can only be done by initiated professionals.

Journalists, as I have tried to show, inhabit an extremely artificial world. I am increasingly troubled by the thought that I have spent all my working life in a single London-based news organisation with a very special ethos. I am not sure that anyone should be admitted to journalism – or to the church or to the teaching profession – without having had some experience elsewhere; or that anyone should be allowed to spend more than, say, ten years as a journalist in one continuous stretch. Perhaps journalism ought to be a part-time occupation (though my union will not thank me for that suggestion). Frankly I think there is less mystery and trained skill in the job than most journalists like to pretend. It is not the craft that is difficult, given the inclination to it; what is so exacting is the way of life.

I am in favour of de-mystifying journalism – and every other occupation. All of them have their everyday holiness and I would not expect a Christian journalist to be any more diligent, prophetic or well-informed than any other craftsman. What his Christianity should do for him is to help him withstand the dehumanising, cynical effects of his experiences – to give him his sense of vocation, his very reason for being a journalist at all. For me, the knowledge of God incarnate among men, of the Christ in every man, is perfectly reconciling, the source of a certain optimism in spite of everything.

118

Still I am concerned that we in the media distress people needlessly with what we publish, and I believe the sin of over-simplification is often the result of our efforts to sell people information that most of them do not really need. We forget, at times, that it is not compulsory to be well-informed about every aircraft that crashes in Ladakh or every lightning strike in Liverpool. Some of the most useful people I know do not follow the news at all, and I would recommend to everyone the taking of an annual holiday from the news: a couple of weeks in the wilderness without radio, newspaper or television. When you return to civilisation, you will find you have missed very little of any real importance to your life.

Certainly the media won't have achieved anything. For they are not, in themselves, creative. What they do is to affect the *acoustics* of society, the lighting, the way we see and hear things. They act as resonators, amplifiers, public address systems, spotlights. But in themselves they are sterile and empty. They are bridges waiting for somebody to cross them, mirrors waiting for something to reflect, and those who make their living in them are constantly waiting about for something or somebody to make use of them. It is up to Christian people not to sit back complaining that good news never comes. It is for Christian people to rise up and make, utter, do that good news, to make use of the media and befriend those who work in them.

The churches themselves must bear some of the responsibility for less desirable features of the media; for too often the churches have turned their backs upon them, spoken their message inward to themselves, and left the media to less admirable but far better organised bodies with no inhibitions about publicity. Seeing our Lord did not hesitate to publish his message loud and clear, why should his church? Any branch of it that does feel bold enough to use the mass media should, I think, cultivate four essential factors. The first is openness. The church must overcome its exclusiveness and its distaste for what it tends to regard as the vulgar, rowdy unscrupulous trade of journalism. It should be frank about its own processes, for, after all, what secrets can the church have to conceal? And if it does, from time to time, feel betrayed by the unevangelised media, it has very clear instructions from its Master about the number of times it should forgive and try again. For it must also cultivate the factor of personality, selecting the right people to speak for it (a charism, surely) and commisioning them in turn to win the understanding and confidence of journalists.

A very large part of an information officer's usefulness lies in the factor of facilities. He will do journalism and the church more service by answering questions than by posting handouts. He must be available to provide the right help at the right time, and speedily. His notebook must be full of names and references and telephone numbers, and he must be able to supply texts and transcripts to people too busy or too idle to make their own.

Finally comes the factor of topicality, of relating the work of the church to the lives of ordinary people. To anyone who suspects this is an example of the Marxist–liberal plot to politicise religion, I must reply that it is the only way I know to resist the politicising of life as a whole, which seems to me the real danger. My object is to sanctify life, and not to let religion be locked away in a gilded Gothic cage, only to be opened on Sundays. There should be no gulf, I believe, between experience and religious experience for anyone whose life is guided by faith.

I wish, then, to see journalism sanctified, too, as it pursues its impossible quest for the Holy Grail of truth, a truth we seek hopelessly to capture in the clumsy, wide-meshed net of language. At times we are tempted to despair. But language itself is a sacrament, consecrated by our Lord's own handling of it. Nevertheless, I make so bold as to end with the words of the pagan Confucius:

> If language is not used rightly, if what is said is not what is meant, then what ought to be done will be left undone, morals and art will be corrupted, justice will go awry and the people will stand about in helpless confusion.